"As It Is The Truth!"
by Judge Anna von Reitz

Maine Republic Free State
3 Linnell Circle
Brunswick, Maine 04011

www.mainerepublicmailalert.com

"As It Is The Truth!"

"As It Is The Truth!"

by Judge Anna von Reitz

Contents

"Ye shall know the truth, and the truth shall make you free." — John 8:32

"As It Is The Truth!"

Anna Maria Wilhelmina Hanna Sophia:
Riezinger-von Reitzenstein von Lettow
a.k.a
Judge Anna von Reitz

Blogtalk Radio

http://tobtr.com/9047611

Brillance In Commerce
Radio Show Episode 12

July 20th, 2016

Welcome to Everyone.
And we have some very exciting guests today. This is Tom Sensarmont, your host, and we have today Anna von Reitz and Royal Solomon and all kinds of exciting topics and people and ideas, good fortune and wisdom and blessings to share with you today.

The testimony of
Guest Speaker Judge Anna von Reitz
begins at minute 47:54.

"As It Is The Truth!"

1

Brilliance In Commerce
--- *Episode 12* ---

Welcome to Everyone. July 20, 2016. Brilliance In Commerce.

And we have some very exciting guests today. This is Tom Sensarmont, your host, and we have today Anna von Reitz and Royal Solomon, and all kinds of exciting topics and people and ideas, good fortune, and wisdom and blessing to share with you today.

So, I want to start with checking with a question that has been raized. Later in the show we will have questions and answers. In this case I've unmutted a 907 Area Code. Which is Alaska? I'm wondering. Is that you Annna?

LISTENER: No. This is a listener.

OK. Very good. Thank you. And welcome to the show. I was looking for Anna's phone number.

Welcome to the show. And we're going to get started shortly here. And we'll move on and look for, uh, . . . all of our guests today . . . We're going to be talking about gold and banking and individual soverignty and restoration of the American Republic. We're going to be talking about building up one's asset column and there's all kinds of news and information, class action lawsuits, to give you news about, and I'm going to welcome Royal Soloman. Royal? Are you there?

ROYAL: Yes. I am.

TOM: All right. Welcome to the show. Glad you're here. And everyone. I wanted to . . . for those of you who are not familiar with

Royal in Hawaii, based on Lulu, and the bringer of the Golden Age. She's been a gatherer of freedom and liberty to many thousands of people, taught a forgiveness method that goes far beyond Holoman Pono and those who are experienced in higher consciousness and well educated in the Galactic perspective of what really is happening on the planet and understand how important our creations of the dawn are, arising now on the history of the earth ascension are, and so we have the blessing of seeing a mystery arising of inner and outter physical and spiritual health, and healthy, worldly and divine, temporal manifestation, and eternal realization.

Royal has some friendship developing with Anna. And so Anna and Royal are working together in building a Bank and in collaborating on helping everyone get their gold accounts set up, and that's why we have a duel affinity of the two, speaking today on the show.

Royal has read hundreds of the most profound spiritual and scientific books in the world and ecliped them all with cosmic conditions of his own from the inner light. Those close to him have seen many synchronicities and miracles, and we're also watching the unfoldment of the new monetary system on this planet aligned with honor, aligned with the new principles that will govern the coming age when corruption is left in the past. History is going to record how the dark ages are replete with negativity, and now positivity, generousity, philanthropy, beneficence, honesty, openness, fairness, enlightenment, oneness, all of the fellowship of the stream of love, universal love, unconditional love that is at the essence of all religious, spiritual paths, philosphical traditions, and will be the basis of a new level of prosperity and peace.

And Royal and Anna are two of the people helping to make this happen. So I wanted to ask Royal, how did you first come to know Anna, and how did you get aligned with her? I know a lot of the people listening today are readers and followers of Anna von Reitz and may not be as familiar with you. So your informing them of how you came to know her and collaberate with her might be interesting.

ROYAL: Well it was very simple. A lot of people were doing research when I fell upon a research group when I was in California, and they had a lot of her materials. I was very very impressed with her and impressed with the depth of the research and the global scope of what she was doing and I just felt compelled to call her and talk to her and praise her and thank her for everything she was doing and ask her if she needed any assistance in some of the areas that I could help her with, and we formed a bond that way.

TOM: Right. Beautiful. And you know that she has gone a little beyond many of the other patriots in the country and that she's extended her work to the international level, gone beyond little skuffles and legal battles and local scales, and extended it into the national and international scale, even reaching, reaching to the Vatican, and so crossing over the boundaries of governments to religion and engaging at the highest levels of administration on this planet with tremendous actions, as well as intelligence, penetrating to the core of the problem and implementing the legal actions and filings, and education the people needed to bring about the solutions.

And you've done similar things, you've done similar work. There's a very great alignment and parallel synchronicit resonance, between the two of you and you also have an understanding of gold and Anna is now bringing gold into the picture. Would you like to talk about gold a little bit?

ROYAL: Well, gold has got a history on this planet as far back as man has known. And it's interesting that this planet goes in cycles starting with the Golden Age and then we go into the Silver Age, and Bronsze Age, the Iron Age, and then it goes slowly back into the Golden Age, so when you look at cycles, gold does play and internal part of everything. And gold is sacred. A lot of people don't know too much about the Galactics, The Ascended Masters, and that sort of thing, but if you really did some research in that you'd find that gold actual creates and engineers our cells. The cells of the higher beings are actually made out of gold. So there's a real significance to gold, in the Galactic empire.

By Judge Anna von Reitz   9

Gold is alive, and everything we touch is alive. People don't think gold is a living thing but in reality it just has a shell on it. If you were to break it down into its smallest components you'd see that it is very very much alive, and that's where it becomes spiritual.

In the third density it looks like a polished metal but once you take that shell off it's very slive, it basically looks like light. It's an entity. It has intelligence. And what's interesting about our cells, our cells themselves have receptor sites, that they can actually partake of gold. Just like we can partake of food.

Our cells have receptor sites that actually accept light as a food. So it's interesting that they are there, and if gold is taken to the proper form you can actually utilize it as a divine food. Actually being gold, this whole thing was gold because in the end gold is the key to allowing us to the ascension.

So that kind of brings us to where we are today. When we look at where we are today . . . the main mission today with all of us is to actually acquire gold, put gold back into our hands. Use gold as a medium of spending between our entities, our countries, our governments.

Gold will be the united factor that unites the planet together, like we look at the Paris Treaty that was just signed. Every country in the world now just signed a pact that they would go back to goldbacked currencies within the next six months. China last month on the eighteenth [June 18] actually started issuing their first gold yuans.

So we're seeing a tremdous transition back to gold and that's what happens in the beginning of the Golden Age. We're now, what, 4-1/2 years into the Golden Age [which began in 2012], and what makes our Golden Age golden is that people recognize the superiority, the power, that gold is and how it has the ability to unite the world in peace.

And more importantly, when everything is said and done, that evetually we'll come to find out the true purpose of gold, and the true purpose of gold is obviously that it is a divine food which allows for the ascension of all mankind, the animals, plants, and the planet itself. So it's a very sacred element in the universe and it has a very sacred purpose, just like it has here on earth. You still their Thomason?

TOM: Yes. Thank you. Beautiful. Facinating. There is a lot everyone, ladies and gentlemen, that is unfolding here today on the call, that is the reason for this session, that will relate to you right now personally. Hm. I wanted to bring up something that I've been observing, Royal, in many people.

I'm speaking to that new thing that is unfolding, they're waiting for the big picture, the global currency reset or some kind of thing, or they're considering joining us and working with us, a lot of them are saying, well, I'll do that when I have the money, and they keep putting off the future. When I have the money then I will do it and they keep like holding a carrot in front of their noses on tomorrow, tomorrow, next week, next month, next year, when such and such happens, and until then, I'm going to sit back and just wait.

And this has been going on month after month, year after year, for millions of people, and I encounter it every day, and I think you do too. I'm wondering if you can speak to that mindset, and what the difference is with those who are co-creating the Golden Age.

ROYAL: I hear the same thing. I see the same thing. But when you look at the cosmic plan, the plan goes in stages. And when you come into a Golden Age, especially the plan for right now, the plan is to get gold back into the hands of the pople. So it's not just gold, the divine plan is to ensure that gold gets into the hands of the people. Gold stabilizes our local community, Gold stabilizes our states and national communittees. And gold at once will stabilize the global economy. And everything is headed that way. And if you're awake, and aware of who you are, and what your place is on the planet, the most important thing that you should do, for the time, is get involved, and helping people learn about gold, especially as a currency.

Even Fiat cripto currency are becoming popular, they're so Fiat — they're not based on gold and everything. So we actually have an opportunity to share and help people get back into the gold standard. Get back into the gold fusion, or undersnding what gold is and educate the people of you freinds.

Fiat currency is worthless. What is an electronic credit worth? I mean, how many people have IRA's and 401K's and mutual funds, and they have CD's, and their savings account, earning 1 or 2% a year.

It's not even safe in our banks. So there's a tremendous opportunity to teach them that there is a safe way on the planet to save their money, and that's alway been gold. So I encourage people to get involved and become a part of what we're doing, and supporting Anna. Anna truly wants to build a maga bank, but it requires a lot of us.

TOM: Yes. It requires a lot of us. We are builintg together ... Go ahead.

ROYAL: So we have an opportunity to support Anna. Support the ushering in of the Golden Age and be a participant, rather than just standing still and not doing anything, and waiting for everyting to happen.

If in 10 to 15 years we can look back and say, if someone asks us and says, what did you do at this auspicious time, wouldn't it be nice to say that, I did everything I could. I did the most important thing which is to get gold into the hands of the people, to teach them about Fiat money, to help stabilize the planet, our communites, and such in the Golden Age, and be a participant, and working and participating, in this officious time we live in, and being a part of it personally.

TOM: You were talking about the spiritual resume, but what goes on the resume?

"As It Is The Truth!"

ROYAL: Well each one of us have got to realize that we are all spiritual beings. This is not where we really live. This is not really our home. We're here for school. We have a different home that we all live in. We come here for school. There're billions of planets in the universe. So we're here for a reason and purpose. We came here for a reason and purpose.

We just didn't come here to play video games, and watch our playbook, and go out and play hockey, or swimming, or whatever it is. We came here to complete a mission at this point of time which is to usher in the Golden Age and stabilize the planet. I came here to stabilize the world and I completed my mission. And that goes on you spiritual resume.

You want something to be powerful on your spiritual resume. And we have the opportunity to do that right here, now. Yeah, I mean, um, there is a kind of attitude that, well, I'm going to sit around and read emails and watch websites and blogs, and listen to conference calls, and kind of watch the global scale.

People are facinated with this global change taking place. Did you ever hear that funnuy saying about, there are those who make things happen, there are those who watch things happen, and then there are those who wonder what happened?

TOM: How much is that paying you?

ROYAL: What everyone needs to know, is that we now have the greatest vehicle on the planet. Anna has finally been endorsing it, thanks to her genius — and you were saying she was a scientist. So in addition to being a legal genius, she has also been a scientist for many decades. And with her penatrating intellect she was able to see that this gold business that is based out of Germany, that we are now colaborating with, can make everyone properous and make every one independent of the international system, with no reporting, can make one independent, actually and legally, and pull the rug out from under the slave masters.

There's another point too. Many people in this audience have been fighting battles — court battles, legal battles, identity battles, mortgage foreclosures, tax issues, debt issues, tyranny, abusive local, national, and state governments, and so many court cases being engaged in.

There a lot of lawyers and legal eagles on this show today. Can we speak to what Anna, and you and I, are offering in the way of joining us, in the way of the gold business, and gold consultation, where you become an arranger, where you become an orchestrator, where you become and introducer of parties, in you neighborhood, or anywhere on the planet that you make known to us, and we will help you bring them into the gold business as family, and create families secure with gold accounts of their own, and therefore move the economy more commercial, out of the old fiat systems that are the source of all the tyranny, and thus unplug, as it were, the power from that which is causing the corruption in the first place.

It's kind of like going to the source of the problem, rather than . . . suppose you have a poisonous tree in your front yard, or some kind of moss, and your just trying to attack it on the outside edges, just trying to defeat it on the surface. If you go to the source, if you go to the root of it, it's gone, finished, forever.

And now a new paradigm can dawn. This is what Anna is getting involved in. What we are involved in, and we are going to the source by pulling the rug out from this dispensation, the financial and monetary dispensation that has been existing. The other thing is that you, Royal, have been speaking with Anna about, and working together on, is with her bank and with the things you're involved in, actuallly laying the foundation for a new Global monetary system.

ROYAL: Well, that's where we are. We come here with a purpose and a mission but we're not just humans. There's more to us. And if you realize it, the universe is alive. The universe . . . if you can connect with the universe, the universe has a part in this and will support and assist you, and you will realize that the only real enemies are the enemies that you perceive are enemies, for technically they are really not enemies, and once you take a more Galactic perspective, then you can look down upon the planet . . . I tried to tell a lot of my friends, that I can work from the bottom up, which a lot of people try to do, but it's a lot easier for me to work from the top down.

And I look at what's happening at the top levels of government, and the top levels of finance, and I've been able to acquire professionals and experts in all those areas, and basically do it from meditation.

I meditate every day, as you know, Thompson, and I meditate on what is needed for this planet, and what I can do to kind of support it, and it's like magic. The people are talented, the engineers, the specialists, they're coming to me to work with me, because they see that attitude that I have, the honor, they see the perspective, and they understand that it's time now to take over our monetary system, which has not been in a position to really help the common man, to this point in time.

We all know the bankers are really the problem on a global scale. They just use their fiat money system to link up all of us, our wealth and our families, of our properties and everything else, and that time has come to an end in the Golden Age that reverses everything.

The people actually go back, and we get to be able to access the global funds, and we get to use them for a global purpose. So we had better look at the season too.

I'm looking at the season every single day, and where are we in the stream of time? There's a massive change happening on the planet and everyone of us have the ability to chose a position, to place yourself on the planet and exercise a position, and work in harmony with the divine plan, and that's primarily what I do, understanding that and the universe totally supports it.

Those who know me can see the evidence of that on a daily basis and what happens when you really bond the spirit with the physical and utilize that spiritual sense and the spiritual tools that we have to accomplish the mission while we are here.

TOM: It appears that we all have something in common. You, and Anna, and I, and all the others who are working with us, share a universal view of spirituality, and religion, and that we don't say there's only one religion. We say we honor all religions, we honor all faiths and persuasions, all philosophies, all spiritual paths, as long as basically it's based in universal love, unconditional love.

And that means oneness. It means unity, it means honor, it means to repect, it means fairness, and it means the recognition of the divinity within each person. The godliness within each person. Anna, I know, is this way, any one of the scientific intelligences is this way, any one of the advanced scientific intelligences recognize the unity field, the field of the essence of all things permeating the universe.

And so someone was wondering . . . what is this new universal adminstriation going to be like? How is it going to be fair for all people? Is it going to honor my beliefs and my philosophy. Absolutely Yes! If it's in line with universal intelligence. It doesn't have to be according to a belief system. It only has to be in tune with universal law, with love and honor, oneness, fairness, openness, and unconditionality, the kind of unconditional generosity, philanthropic attitude, a generous benevolent attitude, and certainly getting rid of the vices that have so plagued mankind.

Such as theft and deception, dishonesty, secret black boxes that hide things from people so that nobody can see how you are doing something. All that is gone, in the need for a transparent system.

We have a new paradigm, and a new dispensation of development, of administation, where you and Anna . . . everyone who is on this planet, everyone in America, the great country of the West, who is serving to bring the world in from where it used to be, and people are waking up fast enough finally now with the assistance of the

Chinese and our European friends and other friends around the world bringing down the cirminals.

Maybe you've heard about the gold bounty that was set up by the Chinese Elders for the capture of the various criminals who have been behind a lot of these mass genocides crimes. So as this darkness is disappearing from the planet, those of us who are ready to build a new planet, a new place of properity and peace, are now empowered with tools and resources to make that happen. And let's work together in oneness and unity for that, where nobody is required to subscribe to any particular belief system.

ROYAL: Absolutely 100% Thompson. I couldn't agree more on everything you just said. Now when it comes to oneness, all of us are part of the One. All the planets are part of the One. All of the suns are part of the One. So to think that you're not part of everything is not really thinking it through.

So if we are part of the One then obviously we can connect to the One and become a part of the divine plan. That's kind of what I look at. What is the plan? What are we suppose to do? Where are we in the stream of time? What is the divine plan for each one of us, and participate in it.

And right now the most important thing is about gold. Gold is the secret in the end for everything. It's the secret divine tool that allows for ascension. It allows for us divine communcation. It's the fuel that changes economies. It's the binding force that allows everything to come together and cocreate. And eventually as you morph into who you really are it's gold that powers your body.

So gold really has a special place in the universe. So we have an opportunity right now to work as hard as we can, and to shake everbody up, and when I wake everybody up, I wake everybody up to the fact that gold is a medium of exchange.

Electronic credit is not gold. It's not money. Fiat currency is not money. Really, the only true thing that the world recognizes as money is either silver of gold. And with the Karatbars system, we have an opportunity where we can get involved. We don't have to use our Social Security Number. We have privacy. There's no storage fees for our gold. We can create a business. I mean an incredible business. We can make enough money to take care of our families and have the excitement and fun that we would like to have on this planet. And the Karatbars program offers all of that in spades.

So it's really when you look at all the different factors of how and what it is, it's just a wonderful tool to assist all of us in our growth as spiritual beings. And it's working with Anna, and close with Anna, you know, as intelligent as she is, and structuring it so her bank can prosper through this program, this the foundation of her global bank.

And we will continue to work with her bank and with other banks around the world. This is basically uniting all the sovereign banks together and eventually they will become the master banks of the planet. So there is a master plan working with her too. And we too see that vision and are working very hard behind the scenes to accomplish that, and work with her to make sure that all that comes to pass.

TOM: Until we bring Anna on, it would be nice if everyone could know a little bit more in detail about what the bank is going to be. Can you speak to that?

ROYAL: No, I kind of would rather leave that up to her. She's certainly the expert in that. You know most of us who know Anna, know she's coming from honesty. She's coming from integrity. She's coming from the planetary good. She wants her bank to be special and sacred. And it's a bank that will set the bar. And this is the Key for all of us. We're all setting the bar now.

We're leaving the Iron Age. We're going into the Golden Age. So it's all about honor. It's all about understanding that there is such a thing as dishonor. And we're bringing forth a new bar of creation wih the banks, so they're to serve the people and not just amount for new money. And Anna is really stepping forward, taking the global lead, and really doing that, and that's why I'm supporting her. And I think that if anybody reads her mission statement of what she's doing, they'll be just absolutely honored and thrilled to be a part of what we are doing.

TOM: You're familiar with the Greek genius Buckminster Fuller of the 20th century, who had 48 PHD's. He was the inventor of the Geodesic Dome. He had lots of accomplishments. He was considered, back in the 60's and 70's, as the only person over 30 that the young people could trust.

And he did a calculation, and he's operating that for his Space Ship Earth book in which he calculated the total manmade wealth in the market place and in the banks, and we're not talking about untapped resources under the ground, we're talking about resources already taken out of the eath, and in the market place, goods and services and money in the banks.

He totalled it up to a total dollar amount figure, and then did a simple calculation. He divided it by the world's population and it indicated that every last man and woman and child on the planet would be a millionaire if it were evenly divided. Which demonstrates there was no shortage even back in the 70's.

Do you think that it is not only possible, but can you believe that there are actually some people who do not even think it's applicable, that every person on the planet should have enough, should have good clothing and shelter, and basic transportation and communication and dignity . . . without working? They kind of have this idea that, No, if you don't work for it, you can just starve to death. What's your take on that? What's you view of that?

ROYAL: Well if you look at it in a higher perspecive, in the universe there is no lack. Lack is something that's created here by itself. So it's natual, in a universal concept and universal laws, that there is no lack. There is always plenty. And in this planet people think that there is not enough gold to go around, but that's just not true. There're massive amounts of gold that have been hidden from the conspirators, for this time in the Golden Age. And I've actually had the opportunity to meet and talk to a lot of people who are the trustees of that gold. And they want to use us as a source to bring that gold to the world.

So there is absolutely plenty of gold, there is plenty of wealth. The earth can produce more than enough for every single person. So the concept of not having enough, that's not a concept that the universe even really understands. That's something that's completed by self. And in the Golden Age, every Golden Age, the reason there is gold in them is because, not only is there enough gold for everybody, there is plenty for everybody.

There's plenty for all the animals, there's plenty of peace, there's an excess of time and energy and fun and excitement. So you have to be at this time in history to usher in a Golden Age. And it's really and auspicious time. We're really probably in the most exciting time in this hisroty of mankind, where we can actually in time usher in this Golden Age.

And those of us who are on the inside of the Galactic perspective know that this is a permanent Golden Age. Mother Earth herself is ascending to the 4th dimension, so this is the last time she has to go through, in her process of her cycling. So everything's changing.

Just look at the 60 years that I've been on this planet, the massive changes that have been happening now, are just astronomical on a planetary scale. If you've got access to the Internet and its proper sites, we all know that things are happening at light speed, faster than we could ever even imagine.

So it's time to get serious, It's time to come out and work and have fun and enjoy life and share gold with people, and share the truth about fiat money and do the mass of conversions that have to be done, and truly be a real part, a daily part, an eathly part of this divine transformation that's happening for us all. And that's what I'm here for. I'm excited to be here. I'm excted to do the process. I'm excited to go through it. I'm excited to go and put it on my spiritual resume. And I'm going to work hard every single day that I''m here to accomplish the mission that I intended to do.

TOM: We have a few things in common with you, Royal, and also Anna. Anna has been teaching people how to bring justice in both law and in these remedies to the economic solution.

And the two main wheels of the global cabal enslavement maching have been debts and taxes, as you may know. They get countries in debt. They get individuals in debt. And then they tax people. And you and I have been blessed with success in defeating both of those wheels. And we've been helping many thousands of others to do the same.

And so my offering for everyone present has been **brillianceincommerce.com** which has been helping people defeat that. We have a 100% success rate in cancelling credit card debt without bankruptcy. 100% success rate, no failures in 14 years. And we have trusts which help people move their commerce out of the taxing system, then into an exempt entity so that all your commerce henceforth then is exempt.

So that's in the **brillianceincommerce.com** offering, and now we have Karatbars, which is the gold business based out of Gernany, that has the LBMA certification, which means 99.999% fine 24 karat gold, the highest quality on the planet as authenticated by one of the planet's greatest authority that's internationally recognized, the LBMA authority for certification of the quality of gold.

So this company has instant credibility. And our due diligence has indicated that millionaires and billionaires are entrusting their money with Karatbars. You as a collaborator with Anna or anyone on this show who may not be familiar with Anna who may have been invited by someone else from the show, have the opportunity, if you haven't already, to join with us.

If you are invited by someone from outside the organization of Anna von Reitz, then get with the person who invited you at their Karatbar link, and join with us.

If you were receiving this show information from Anna von Reitz' newsletter, and you want to honor her organization, here is her link at **http://karatgroupsite.com/ameagle1956.html**. So that's **http://karatgroupsite.com/ameagle1956.html**. That is the link to join up with Anna von Reitz in the Kratbars business, and if you were invited by her or her newsletter, go to that link.

If you were invited by someone else at their link, go with them and work with the people who invited you.

Also the American States and Nations Bank website is under development, it's just getting started and that is **www.asanbank.net**. So **'asan'** stands for **American States and Nations** . . . bank. Anna wants a longer domain name to spell it out. I believe there is a longer alternative as well. We'll give these links out again later.

I wanted to address, Royal, the concept — while we're waiting for Anna to come on — of what everyone listening can do to come out of the mindset that, well, I'm waiting for some big global change, or I'm embroiled in a battle in court, or I'm waiting for some kind of money to come in from somewhere, and then I'll do all those things, then I'll get involved in gold.

There is an opportunity right now whereby, starting with little or nothing, you can be an introducer, if you have enough concern in your heart for your neighbors, that you can think, OK, I know some businsess owners, or I know somebody who has a lot of asssets, a lot or resources, and they're afraid. They're afraid of loosing it. They may be afraid of the government taking it over. There's been a lot of asset forfeitures being spread accross the country that has not made the headline news, that is not on PBS, well actually, it is BS which we see. It's not on FOX, it's not in the major media. But it is happening. And you were informed on this, Royal. You've been seeing the news about it.

The government just helps themselves because the Fed's going down. The dollar is no longer accepted worldwide, they're loosing money, they can't make any more money out of thin air, and so they're desperate, and their ship is sinking, so they're grasping.

They're taking people's accounts. Wealthy people are afraid. People holding a retirement pension. How many people with retirement pensions, IRA's and KEOS have had them just disappear because the company failed, they went out of business, they filed bankrupcy, the government confiscated it — something happened.

They can roll their IRA's over into gold. Gold is stable. Karatbars has a system whereby they can do that, and you have met with a company that is pursuant to that. Do you want to speak to this?

ROYAL: Yes. You know, nothing is safe in the banks over here. If the banks get a piece of paper from any government agency, they do it ever day. You can look in your local paper and just see the amount of seizures that are happening on a local basis. There's a local paper over in Hawaii called the Pacific Business News, and there's just page after page, after page every week of massive amounts of seizures.

And this is how the government is surviving right now. They just seize the money and then they can label you for any type of crime they want, and take your money, and throw you in jail. That happens every single day. It's really a dangerous time to have money in banks. Or even money stuffed away someplace where somebody else can take it.

That's why I recommend to the people that if they have CD's, if they have Mutual funds, if they have IRA's that if have saving accounts, 401K's, why not roll them over into something safe, something where you know that it's real money in substance where nobody can take it.

There's no storage fees in Germany in the vaults that the system uses, so we can naturally roll it all over there, and then there is an access to it through MasterCard, and the teaching in the next few month is going to be access to it through the computer so you will be able to move gold anywhere in the world.

So really it's the safest most powerful system in the world at this point of time on the planet. And the fact that you have the MasterCard, so that you can place your gold into your card on the computer, and you can spend that at any store any place where MasterCard is utilized.

So it's really probably the best system that I've ever seen on the planet in this point of time to start the healing of the nation, and it creates the faith that everybody has been looking for. So that's one of the major reasons why I am in this. I help people with that.

TOM: We also provide personal service to everyone. You've got to know . . . this is not just some kind of sales pitch and then we're gone and we're finished. This is actually a family. It is a family of people who care about each other, who care about others, and who are working all day long, every day, just about 7 days a week on the phone, on the Internet helping each other, and we are here for you.

Royal is here. He can consult to you people. Anna is available as much as she can be. Everyone working with Anna with several other affiliates who are associated with Anna, and other people in our group, our family, some who have been in for 2 or 3 years making 6 and 7 figures per month just caring about others and helping families build up their gold reserves in fulfillment of the rich teaching of Robert Kiyosaki that every person should take a portion of what they have coming in each month — whatever it is — and put it aside in something permanent. Something in investment which is stable.

"As It Is The Truth!"

So we are here for you, to consult to you, to provide to you assitance. There is something like a VIP treatment in which everyone gets respect, everyone is treated fairly with love, with care and concern to roll this out. And so perhaps you'd like to speak to that. To the care and concern that this family approach takes.

ROYAL: Well everybody that knows me knows that I've been following and exercising what I believe in. I believe in honor, faith and love, and I believe in respect. I believe in helping and assisting, and to me it is much, much more than money.

We all need money to survive and pay the bills and all sorts of things. But being a con, or stealing money, or trying to steal it from your neighbor, or your friends, or trick them, or deceive them — that's the old paradigm. The new paradigm is to love each other. We stand in honor. We help each other. We never think about harming or cheating, or stealing, or anything.

So to me it's more like a salvation mission where I can actually assist clients getting their money rolled over safely to where it is safe, where they can have access to it, where they don't have to worry about it being stolen, or confiscated by the government, or some type of civil judgment, or even a divorce, or who know what.

At the same time, there's a business here. We can actually make money, legally and honestly and safely, and make enough to provide a wonderful living, much more than a normal job, or any of that type of thing. I could do this full time, but I don't do this full time, because I don't treat it as a job, I treat it as excitement.

Every single day I'm looking forward to helping people and assisting them in accomplishing their goals, and at the same time accomplishing my goals, and at the same time I can assist people like Anna on a higher scale. And assist them in bringing the type of bank, and integrity in the banking system, the loyalty and the honesty, and bring life to the planet. And really truly usher in the Golden Age. And be a part of setting that bar and taking the lead in accomplishing the mission.

MAY: This is May and I'm taking over for Tom, for just a moment. He has connected with Anna, and they're trying to get her on the Radio Show, and we have a few moments here if you can continue talking, that would be good. Can you continue talking about what you were talking about?

ROYAL: Sure. No problem.

MAY: Yah. We're getting her on, but it's taking some directions here. One moment.

ROYAL: Well one of the most important things that I'm excited about is having a business that you don't have to spend a tremendous amount of money to put it together. Business today costs . . . if you do a franchise . . . it could cost hundreds of thousands of dollars, and millions of dollars to put a franchise together.

And you don't have to pay rent. You don't have to pay for a staff. You don't have to do insurance, and just a narrative of things. It's unbelieavable what it costs to run a business now-a-days. Yet with Kratbars, you can start with just a few hudred dollars.

You don't have to worry about a space. You don't have to worry about having a staff. Because everybody involved with the Karatbars system becoms your staff, all of this is basically for free. We all will help you out. You don't have to pay rent. In Germany they take care of everything over there, so there is no rent for you.

So you can venture out in a business on a shoe-string and build it into something powerful. And I have incentive to do that. I have worked with people every day and in every scale. You know if they've just got $300 dollars and are first time coming in and purchasing gold, in a package, and getting started, I treat that person with just as much respect and honor as I do the billionaires honor on that basis.

"As It Is The Truth!"

So it's really a wonderful program, and depending on where they are, and assist them in accomplishing their mission and their goals. So it's very rare to have a business like this, and at the same time it's also a private business. They don't require any Social Security Numbers to sign up. There's not any type of government reporting to any government. We're in 122 countries already so we can do a business worldwide. I've got people all over the world working with me and because calling doesn't really cost anything any more, all that expense is eliminated so we can truly have a global business working right now out of our home.

So just that alone, and also to be able to support people like Anna, and to assist in and helping ushering in the Golden Age, and setting up new types of banking, and banking systems that will truly benefit the people, we are honored to be a part of this, and work with people to accomplish their mission. It's really an opportunity of a lifetime.

TOM: Anna. I believe you are on, and we have you unmutted. Would you like to say Hi to everybody? Well, Anna. Are you there? Hello. Are you there?

ANNA: Yes.

TOM: Hi Anna. You're finally on the air. Welcome. Welcome. We've been introducing you and singing your praises and laying out the red carpet and kind of paving the way for you. And thank you everyone for listening and for your patience. But Anna, we want to listen to you for awhile, and see what you have to share with us.

ANNA: Well, first my apologies. I have actually been listening to you guys for the last hour thinking, well gee, they're letting me off easy. But anyway. We finally got settled with the technical things worked out, and I'm sorry that that happened, but I have been listening to the conversation. And maybe I could throw in a few things about the American States and Nations Bank that we're building.

The testimony of
Guest Speaker Judge Anna von Reitz
begins at minute 47:54.

"As It Is The Truth!"

2
Testimony of Judge Anna von Reitz

Basically, banking is something that everbody has a right to engage in, and in fact that is guaranteed by law. Banking is something in which everyone has a right to act as a banker if they wish to, especially under the provisions of Article 10 of the Consitution, which is an agreement with the federales. The states and the people reserve all of the rights that are not exclusively delegated to the federal government.

And if you read the Constitution you'll see that it is an agreement between the states and the federal entities, but the people are not part of that agreement except in a secondary subjected standing. We are mentioned in the Preamble. We are mentioned in Article 10. We are mentioned in Amendment 7. But we are not bound by anything in the Constitution.

We have the ability to retain our full sovereignty, and it's only our fault that we don't. We can give it away, but it can't be taken from us.

And essentially, some hoodnicks, no good hoodnicks, got in here and worked a fraud scheme that has resulted in the American people being deprived of the exercise of their sovereignty for many years. But that, none-th-less, doesn't make it right. And fraud has no statute of limitations.

So in terms of commerce there is absolutely no doubt that the individual Americans who reclaim their state and national status — that is their birthright status — become nationalists of the State of the Union, such as Californians, Virginians, Origonians, Washingto-nians, Wisconsinites, Minnesotans, etc.

If you are reclaiming that status by statehood and many assumed statuses as a United States Citizen, or a Citizen of the United States, you can exercise your sovereignty to a plumb. You don't have to worry about any challenge from the federal government.

You can open your own bank — and so we're opening our own bank. We've reclaimed our national status as birthright people of the sovereign states and in that capacity we can operate an international bank.

We can trade or we can engage in commerce and the essential difference is that trade is private and lawful, and commerce is public, and based on commercial paper.

Strictly speaking, corporations deal in commerce, whereas people deal in actual money, and that's one of the conundrums that we faced in figuring out what those fraudsters did and how they did it.

They arbitrarily named corporate franchises after us. They infringed upon the copyright of our name that we never intended to give them and which our mothers and fathers never intended to give them.

So we have a tortuous copyright infringement claim against the British Crown and against the British Government.

But in any event, now that we know about all of this we're in a position to take charge of our lives again; take charge of our property again; and to object to the actions and the presumptions of those various foreign governments and foreign corporations that have sought to enslave and make use of us for their own benefit.

So in one's sovereign capacity, having done some paperwork, and contacted the public saying otherwise, you can operate a bank.

So the America States and Nations Bank is basically a 3-part institution. It has a bank depository for the purpose of receiving assets that the Americans are owed, that can then be deposited and held by the bank depository. And then there is an International Bank that can interface with the CITS System which is the gold trading system which the Chinese have launched — or with the Swiss system which is the currenct system for making transactions in the fiat room.

I think it's important for everyone to understand that there are two completely diffent systems, the Forex, and there's the Iex. The Forex is the system platform for making fiat transactions, and the Iex is the new soon-to-be-introduced system for making trades and transactions in lawful money, and it's necessary for international banks to be able to translate their interests into both systems.

And the powers that be, who have a vested interest in continuing to force people to use fiat currency, based on commercial notes and that sort of thing, are trying to stop Americans essentially from participating, and are installing a more global economy and foreclosing on our ability to trade in lawful money, but they're not going to be able to do that.

So that in essence is the position of the soverign bank to be able to interface those systems and be able to do transactions globally for people. And that's another part of the bank. And the 3rd part of the bank is the actual state banks.

Now this is a little confusing, as many of these things are, because there's been a deliberate effort over a long time to confuse the identities of things.

We've seen that over and over again, when they've tried to confuse people about which state they are talking about. Because I can see that there's a state of mind, a state of being, there's a state of state of almost anything you can think of, and they deliberately mess things up so that it is hard to even talk about which state are you talking about.

When we talk about our states — the states that we live in that have rocks, and trees, and gravel, we're talking about the state in its most elemental organic sense. And the names of those states are always in all small letters.

I know that sounds strange but that's the way it is. That would be "oregon", in all small letters if you're talking about the actual factual organic state. Those states that are inhabited, where the people live, are represented by unincorporated states, and those have been named according to a differnt convention, which is Texas State, California State, and so on.

Each one of our organic states, and they're States of America, are nation-states. They're political entities, but they are States on the Sea and Nations on the land. And so it's a jurisdictional thing where you're both a state and a nation, and that nation and that state has a natural name, like California, Oregon, or Texas. OK?

So when we call it the "America States and Nations Bank", we're making claim to serve both the land jurisdiction and the sea jurisdiction. And we can do that because We-the-People are not hindered by the Constitution. We're protected by it. Its guarantees are to us, not the other way around, because as individual sovereigns we can do what the federal government will not allow any states or organizations to do.

Now when we do this on a state basis, where we start a California State Bank, that bank is limited because it is a party to the Constitution, but it can trade in any form of lawful money. It can even mint its own coinage, issue its own gold backed certificates, and basically establish its own bench mark, as well as it can interface with other state banks and form associations of state banks, because the other state banks could do a joint venture with the California State bank. Or the Alaska State bank could have an agreement with all of the other sister banks of the nation, that are going to form a National Coinage Act revision to make an American National Currency.

So there are a lot of things we can do that are allowable under the

"As It Is The Truth!"

Constitution, and we just need to get busy and get ourselves ready and get our own ducks in a row, do our own declarations, make sure our own statuses are corrected, and go forward.

TOM: *Anna, I heard that the State of North Dakota has a very stable economy because it exercises its right to its own currency.*

ANNA: It can. Well, ya. If you look at the Constitution it says that the states are absolutely forbidden to issue any kind of currency except gold and silver coins, within the federal state relationship, but that isn't talking about the states relationship with the rest of the states, it's not talking about its relationship with the people. So, ya. They can issue their own currency. They can have their own state bank even though they are a "State-of" organization. That's allowable. But they're restricted from having a National, I should say, an International currency, because the United States government is supposed to be providing that for us.

TOM: *And so, will the American States and Nations Bank have an international currency?*

ANNA: We may, but we would have to, as a practical matter, have a consensus with the other states.

TOM: *What about denominating its money in the Karatbar notes — these one world currency notes woven with gold and with the grams of gold printed on it?*

ANNA: Well, you could possibly do that. There are so many different things. We could contract with a provider — like Karatbars — to mint our own currency in, and have an America States gram-card, or there are a lot of different ways addressing this in making the products available.

I think a lot of people have thought about money in a kind of superstitious and silly way and have not thought of money as a product. But all these diffent things are products. They're consumer items just like anything else. And if you don't want to use FRNs, you can use something else. People have to become more sophisticated and they have to be better consumers in terms of monetary products.

TOM: *What would be the main benefits of say, the average customer of the American States and Nations Bank, as distinguished from other banks?*

ANNA: Well, I think there are a lot of advantages, because many of these existing banks have locked themselves into contractual and franchise agreements that don't allow them to operate in a private way, that don't allow them to actually use lawful money. They've also, by and large, made agreements that force them to practice unlawful conversion against private people.

When you walk into a bank the very first thing they offer you is a "personal" account. And most people hearing that think, OK, "personal" — that means my own, my own account, right? My own individual account makes sense.

But that's not what it means.

Back in the 1860s the Congress pulled a fast one, and for federal purposes changed the meaning of the word "person" to mean "corporation". So when you walk into a bank which is a federal franchise under the FDIC Scheme, and they ask you if you want a "personal" account and you stupidly nod your head, yes, that means that you're signing up for a corporate franchise account, and that means that they're going to ask you for a Social Security Number to prove that you're a "franchisee". And then, everything that you put into that account belongs to the government. It belongs to a government franchise. And you have the authority to write checks on that account, but everything that you deposit is a 100% gift to that government franchise.

And that's why when the IRS starts bullying people, and they go in there and look at bank accounts, and they threaten to start this garnishing and all the rest of the stuff that they do, what they're doing is they're bringing a charge against a government franchise corporation, and they're also counting every dollar that you deposit — "voluntarily" — to their franchise as "income".

Income is a term that is uniquely . . . It's unique in its form of legal and accounting meaning. Income is an accrual of a corporation. Private Property is what people accrue.

So right at the moment that they start talking about an "income" tax, a light should go on in your brain, and you should say, OK! Your're talking about a corporation making "income". They're not talking about me, Joe Average, and my wages or earnings.

But, you see, because people don't bother to look up the legal meaning of words, and because frankly, a lot of this stuff, the real skullduggery, has been hidden in reams of ugly historical documents, 150 years old now. This has been in this horrible, hiddeous, duplicitus "dopedom" that is setup, geared and intended to fleece us blind.

But we now have the goods on them.

We know what they've done. We know how they did it. We know who did it. We know when they did it. We know why they did it. And we have all of the proof that any reasonal being would ever need to conclude, that yes, we were swindled. And I do mean fraud in the broader sense of that word.

TOM: *So it sounds like ASNB would not have any involvment in that kind of design. It would now have a design where you would absolutely own the account that you open and you would own the assets in it, if you were the depositor and the customer of it. Right?*

ANNA: Right. Totally private. Your own account. No government interference. No government franchisee. In fact, it's part of our planning for the bank. What we're doing, you know, everybody has these lousy numbers and all these systems they have to interface, so what we're looking at is setting up the double blind, maybe even a triple blind system where when you come into the bank and you want to set up your own accounting system you get an individual what is called an ILBN, Individual Living Being (identity) Numeric code that is yours and unique on the entire planet. And that nobody knows, that nobody uses but you. And you have a *public* code that you can use to make up a license plate for your car, your trademark, your property.

But you also have a *private* code and *key* code that are yours so that nobody can get into your accounts or bother your business or do anything to you at all, in our bank.

And there's alway the pendulum swing

Things went so far, so Communistic, so crazy back in the 30's when FDR went gung-ho on this, and really started the Social Security System and all of that crap, but now we're going back the other way, and we're using their own technical identity and their own system against them that they used, the numerical system, the Social Security System, as an escrow key and they basically took all of our private stuff and made it public stuff. And now we're going to turn that around and use the same system to protect people's privacy.

TOM: *A lot of people may be wondering, Oh, this sounds wonderful, but how can it be protected from those very feds who have been so zealous in attacking good things. How would this bank be protected from them?*

ANNA: Well, a lot of the federal corporations are going to go away, because the Crown gets into this, and they're going to be liquidated. And that's going to take a lot of wind out of their scheme, their crime misfits. They're not going to be able to go bully playing around, in harming Americns any more — and it's coming fast.

I just got word of over — almost one million organized people signing up to be federal marshals, and going through federal marshal training. There are three million government employees, basically, if you don't count some of the agencies, and we've already got one-third people signed up to act as federal marshals. And to enforce the public laws, and stop all this.

So this is someething that's peaceful. It's lawful. It's unarguable. It's the truth. And those corporations that have been here missbehaving and indulging in fraud, and extortion, and racketeering, against Americans, are going to have a real hard time operating that way anymore.

And that goes for the court system too. Because they're just plain out and out replacing the military tribunals with American courts. American common law courts that serve American State Nationals instead of US Citizens.

What happened is that after the Civil War they had the situation where the Northern states had been bankrupted by Lincoln and the Southern states were in ruin. OK? So nobody was minding the hen-house. Everything was in chaos.

In desperation Abraham Lincoln turned to his Generals and gave them the authority to protect the nation's money. And he also gave them the General Orders 100, the Lieber Code, to protect our borders and property, and there were all sorts of rules they had to operate under.

The Lieber Code has never been withdrawn. It's never been inactivated. The Department of Defense is still under the Lieber Code. And that's because the Civil War never really ended. The Civil War has been going on for 160 years. We just were not told that, and it was not supposed to affect us.

What happened, as we all know, was there was an Armistice at Appomattox in April of 1865. Lee's Army surrendered to Grant's Army. Hook Law. Everybody's happy.

Subsequently to that, President Andrew Johnson made three public declarations saying, "We're at Peace on the land", "Peace on the land", "Peace all over the land". This is great, right? But there was no Peace Treaty. There was no official Peace Treaty ever ending the Civil War.

The United States remained at war in the international jurisdiction of the sea. And it's been at war in the international jurisdiction of the sea ever since. So that is what created the problem, where our country has been kept constantly embroiled in war after war, after war, after war, after war.

And these idiots in Congress who declared war had no authority what-so-ever to declare war. And in fact all those things they've engaged in are nothing more than glorified "police actions". A corporation does not have the authority, or ability, to declare war. And they've been operating exclusively as a corporation since 1868.

You see the problem. These people are in it so deep in terms of their unlawful actions that just being associated with this government is a problem. I don't care if you're a file clerk, it's so bad that these mongrels have done this to the unsuspecting Americans, after doing eveything possible to create the impression that we've been at peace. And essentially when a President stands up in public and makes three public declarations — big announcements — that you're at peace. That's a contract.

Andrew Johnson made a contract with the American people, that the land jurisdiction is at peace. That was his authority to us. And it's been great all these years, except that in the international   jurisdiction [of the sea] we've been at constant war.

That's where the Trading with the Enemy Act comes in. The War Powers Act. All these illegal actions. All these . . . you know, the Draft. The Draft, what a completely criminal, completely unsupportable action. And they drafted millions of men in World War II. They drafted hundreds of thousands in Korea. And they drafted more hundreds of thousands in Viet Nam.

And 55,000 of people in my generation died in Viet Nam because of wounds afflicted in Viet Nam, or because of being taken as POWS in Viet Nam. They were conscripted, they were press-ganged, they were enslaved against their will. For the most part, anybody who was drafted wasn't standing there volunteering.

So, you know, when you think about it, these people need to be arrested. And no doubt, some of them are just plain stupid, and didn't know that they were doing anything wrong. But you can bet that at least a significant portion of them DID know full well that they were doing something wrong.

And especially those that were juris doctors, the guys . . . how many members of Congress are there who are lawyers, of the United States Congress, that is. They're lawyers. They have to know the law. They have to study this stuff, and you can bet that some of them knew full well what they were doing. And are just doing it now as profit mongering, greedy nasty vermin.

So and then we get to the Titles of Nobility Amendment and all the differnt Constitutions that have been palmed off on us. When you really start looking at it, when you really start understanding how they named things very similarly, so that to deceive people, it blows you mind.

Now, when I was growing up, in grade school and Junior High, and in High school, the only Consitution that I ever saw, or ever heard of, was call the *Constitution OF the United States of America*. And I'm sure that for most of you that's what you grew up with too. It was published in 1868 by a corporation calling itself *the United States of America*. They just didn't add the *Inc*.

And so this document is not the actual Constitution. The actual Constitution which is called the original equity contract by the Vatican and by the British Monarch and all the other party-hearties, it's call the *Constitution FOR the united States of America,* and the word *"united"* has a small *"u"* meaning that that word was being used, not as a title, not as a proper name of anything, but as an adjective describing, *States of America.*

So this is going to kind of come as big news to everybody, but the name of this country, as a confederated establishment under the Articles of Confederation, is *States of America.* And it alway has been. No *"united"* anything about it.

Well so, anyway, there are all kinds of Constitutions and if you want proof of what I just told you, you can go on the Internet and look up the oath that your, not really your, but those persons in Congress who are supposed to be representing you. Now if you look up their oath, you will see that they take their oath to something called the *Constitution of the United States* — no *"of America"* about it, just the *Constitution of the United States.* And how many of us have even seen the *Constitution of the United States?*

There has been so much chicanery going on. So many deceptive names used to accrue people such a shell game that it is absolutely shameless.

You'll have to forgive me. I get a little bit compassionate about all this.

TOM: *Ha, Ha. That's beautiful. Heh. Heh.*

ANNA: Ya. It's shamful. You know a lot of those corporation are not going to be allowed to conintue. They're not going to be able to do business after something of this magnitude. And they're not going to have an excuse for it. It's all been just greed and control. And more greed, and more control.

And I'm not for the world saying this to harm the Church or to be accusatory toward Catholic people, or anything like that, but it has to be said, and it has to be recognized, that the Church has a fundamental responsibility for this entire mess, because the Church, the Holy See, which is not the Church exactly, but the Holy See came in and actually incorporated a lot of this stuff, and they also put in a lot of the different aspects of it that have been most damaging.

The Internal Revenue Service started out in 1156 as a Crusade Tax. It was called Peter's Pence, and it was a special tax on income that was instituted to help pay for the expenses of the Crusades. So the IRS goes all the way back to the Inquisition. And like the inquisition, and like Peter's Pence, on April 15th is when they collected that, and the Confessions.

So what are you doing when you sign a 1040 form? You're confessing that you owe money — and you're paying it. You're paying your Peter's Pence 1,000 years later — and to the IRS Agents of the Inquisition, then and now.

And if you delve deeply into all of this, you'll find that the United States and its judicial organization is run by the [Catholic] Church. You'll find it if you look up a book called *Principles of Ecclesastical Law* — now doesn't that just warm your heart — wouldn't you just delve into that one, *Ha, Ha, Ha.*

I tell you, I have spent my life reading stuff that would curl your hair in boredom. *Principles of Ecclesastical Law,* it was published in 1894, and it proves beyond a shadow of a doubt that what we think of in the higher forms is statutory law, or common law for the priests, for the emplyees, for the judges.

And *above* that is eccleiastical law, which the Pope wields and which his Rectors, Lord High Chancellors in Equity have complete authority over everything in their Archdiocese. They're the cardinal bishops acting as general cardinals and judicial vicars, or general judicial vicars, and are the ones who are supposed to be making sure that eveything is handled in an equitable and fair and "Christian" manner in the United States for United States Citizens.

But not for *me,* because I am an American State National, thank you very much, but then as United State Citizens, they the "Lord High Chancellors in Equity" are supposed to be making sure that people aren't losing their homes to fraud, to fraudulent claims made by banks that are just over the top.

They're the ones who are supposed to be insuring that people are not breached of custody of their own children. They're the ones that are to make sure that their constituents are not being held in jail for vacuous illegal reasons. And they have fallen down on the job, obviously. They have, instead, been swindling the System ten ways from Sunday. And it's all proven.

The Bank of New York Mellon is the central hub of a human enslavement and racketeering cartel that bogglers the mind.

Vertically the Bank of New York Mellon funds all of the different parts of the states and counties of the federal system. The Bank of New York Mellon owns the federal government, it's agencies, it's 1,031 agencies, it's counties, it's "counties-of", I should say, it's "states-of" which are nothing but franchises of the federal corporation.

And then Laterally, they take your birth certificate bond — and let's discuss what a bond is — a bond is a promissory note, it's like an enslavement indenture, where you, remember back in the days when they had indentured servants, where you would sign up and promise to work for someone for seven years in order to come to America and have a grub stake, that sort of thing — well in this case you're a bonded servant all your life from the time you're in the cradle until you die. And you are working for them, and they are selling your labor, your *promise* of labor on the world market.

So they've enslaved you, and now they're selling the proceeds from that, trading these cusip bonds on the stock market and exchanges. That's what they're doing. And there's a great clearing house for all this.

"As It Is The Truth!"

There's the Depository Trust Corporation, DTC. OK? So the Bank of New York Mellon takes in all these bonds and houses them with the UTC, uses those as securities, and then the proceeds for the [unclear name?] and Company which then forwards it on to the Vatican Bank which launders the money, sends it back to the Canadian Central Bank, and then it gets cycled back to the Bank of New York Mellon. Round and round it goes. And all of this is being founded by slave bonds that are being fostered on people that are friendly "United States Citizens".

So you can see why they are so desperate to entrap everyone and make people believe that they're "United States Citizens" and make them sign up and sign paperwork declaring that they're "United States Citizens", because each one of us, and our property is subscribed to this filthy system and as a result they make millions upon millions of dollars and they enslave us and oppress us and have a handle on us, so they can jerk us around in their own little private tribunals.

And its totally 100% illegal and unlawful, totally. Press-ganging and inland piracy and unlawful conversion of assets, and misscharacterizations of characterization of non-combatant civilians.

Those are war crimes and of huge huge standing. Those are the things that have been outlawed since 200 years ago, and they've been getting away with it, here in American, the quote, unquote, "Land of the Free".

They've been doing it since World War II when Franklin Delano Roosevelt sold us down the drain and so did Winston Churchill. They were both really venal nasty unconscionable men. War criminals. I mean war criminals. No doubt about it.

Now, I'm not saying that Hitler was any better. But if this is the kind of ilk and of person that we have running anything on this planet, we're in trouble. And we better listen up and we better wake up, and everybody better grab an oar and do something about it. And get serious.

RAY: *This is Ray, and I'm taking over for a minute this is so facinating, and its mind boggling, in a way, and heart opening also. Can you share more? Do you have more to share?*

ANNA: Well, there's so much. I mean, anywhere you look. Look at the foreclosure situation. The banks go out and they advertise home loans. Right? And Joe Average is wandering around. And he sees an Ad for a home loan. Right? So naturally he thinks that the bank is advertising to lend him money to buy a home.

That's an entire presumption about the transaction and what "home loan" means. In fact, his bank is advertising for *you* to loan *them* your home. See?

Home Loan. If you will loan them your home they will monetize it and they will benefit the escrow account of the government franchise that operates in your name. Imagine it. Every single one of these loans, those, quote, unquote, "mortgage loans" that we have examined operate the same way. It's a unilateral contract. It is totally missrepresented. An average home mortgage loan has 67 different frauds contracted, that are commonly associated with every single one of them. They are literally not worth the paper they are printed on, except for one fact — all of them are "trade marked".

Every single application that we've looked at is trade marked. And what they do, this is the heart of the whole scam, unbeknownst to you, your signature is very valuable. It is owed unlimited credit and when you make a loan application for one of these "home loans" where you're *giving* the bank your home for them to raise money on for their activities, unbeknownst to you, and unremarked by the bank, undisclosed by the bank, or anyone there standing at the closing table, you're signing a trade marked piece of paper.

For, they seize upon your — they *enclose* upon you. A legal process know as enclosure. They *enclose* your signature. They *steal* your signature. They use you signature then, to create what are called derivatives. Well, derivatives are just like carbon copies of a computer. They just take you signature and they re-produce it wildly, and sell all these things that they create, based on their use and missuse of your signature, and your credit, and they obligate *you* to pay for all of this.

They take that document and trot on down to the nearest US Treasury Window, and they not only get the full amount of the loan that they promised to give you, they also take out the entire amount that would be payable at the end of a 30 year mortgage, and they take that and they increase five of six times the entire amount as you know, if you got a $200,000 dollar loan 30 years from now when that loan matures its going to be more than $1.2 million dollars at least.

So they go down there and they take out the entire amount and they leverage all of that by the bank adding it to them and then, and if that's not enough, right?, they leave you paying this. And it's your home at risk. OK?

And then if that isn't bad enough, they turn around and they saddle you with these monthly mortgage fees that have to be paid for the franchise, for the government franchise. The government franchise wants its cut of this.

So the government franchise actually receives all of your monthly mortgage payments. And that gets fed into a conduit loan. There's no agreement. There's no real estate trust. There's none of that. There's absolutely no IRS filings anywhere, where any of those banks have filed transfer fees of that nature. It's just a huge fraud.

It's another huge, huge fraud against the American people. And, you know, they were so arrogant about it. They were so sure that nobody would ever figure this out, that they wandered down to the taxing office and they patented and trade marked their whole system. This was found out by Merrill Lynch. And then Merrill Lynch hooked Bank of America into it. And it just went straight on down, less and less.

There isn't a lawful mortgage, or anything ever approaching a lawful or legal mortgage in America. They're all acts of legal fraud from the start. Every single one of these banks that's gotten involved in this are guilty, and they've done it under the pretense that they were doing it against "United States Citizens". Not against American State Citizens, but against "US Citizens". Now how do you like that?

They created all these corporate franchises deliberately to abuse them. To use them as debtors and scape-goats. And that's what they have done. They all deserve to be taken out and flogged in the streets.

I don't mean your local banker, he's probably too stupid to know what's going on, I mean, who would imagine such a thing. Right? Not in the wildest dream or nightmares do you imagine what Wall Street has done. What the SCC has failed to do. The guys — like Hank Paulson — they should be sitting in a jail forever for what they've done and for the misery they have caused.

Now at a certain point you just don't let certain people who have caused that kind of mysery . . . you just don't let them loose. They're too much of a danger to society. They're too much of a danger to third parties and little kids about whom they don't care.

I want you to think about this. They attack us when we are babies in our cradle. Long, long before we have any idea about what is going on. They have stolen our identity, taken a copyright out on our name, and are out there selling us in the world market as slaves. And seizing upon our rights, titles to land our forefathers owned and have passed on to us.

You can hardly imagine a more venal, more calamitous, more disgusting system than what's been perpetuated on our soil by these monstors in suits, smiling and glad-handing us, and telling us about Jesus, and about Justice.

This is the biggest fraud of malarkey that you could ever ever imagine. And they talk about Mafiosi being more hard. We're to go after the Mafia Dons? Mafia Dons in their worst day never imagined the kind of stuff that Wall Street and the Vatican have told you.

I mean, do you remember the London Olympics a few years ago, the Winter Olympics in London?

Well, there was a very real thing that happened in a very public manner at the Winter Olympics in London. There was a giant effigy of a dead baby in a coffinlike thing. It's just standing out there, this giant effegy of a dead baby.

And then there were all these hooded figures, you know, like in priests robes, and with hoods over their faces, and they were all marching around, and around, and around the effigy of the dead baby. Well, now we know that the dead baby — they call the infant "decedant" — and that's what they claim we are.

Now being a decedant does not necessarily mean that you're physically dead. It can mean, and in this case does mean that you are presumed to have disclaimed your right to your property. Your right to a nationality. Your right to your name. You are presumed to have disclaimed your right to own land. You are presumed to have disclaimed your right to have ownercship of your home, your car, or anything else. You have supposedly given all this to the main banks and the store front government, these banks they are running, and to the Holy See.

At the end of the day, it's the great mother spider in the center of the web.

Now, I don't want to give anyone the impression that the Church has not done magnificent things for the world too. They have. We wouldn't have public roads. We wouldn't have public bridges. We wouldn't have public schools like we do. We wouldn't have public universities. We wouldn't have public social programs, hospitals, hospices.

By Judge Anna von Reitz   47

The Church has done a lot of this work, and there has been a lot of wonderful, good people who have devoted their lives to the Church. But there is a side of the Church that has been engaged in the secular realm up to its eyeballs for a long long time with disasterous results.

And so its time for a house-cleaning. It's time for a real soulful confession of sin. It's time for everybody on this planet to wake up and realize that we've been sold a real bill of goods. We have been deceived, and lectured in a literally gross way, by people who are supposed to be acting as our trustees who are supposed to be honored men of our communites, who set themselves up as the creme de la creme, as the most educated and the finest and the richest, and the most intelligent, who are actually nothing but a bunch of rats. Vermin.

TOM: *Anna. There was an ever enlightened Master from India, named Osha, who said that all the evil in the world can be traced to two classes of people, the politicians and the priests. And he was persecuted for saying that of course and kicked out of countries, and so forth. But he was obstinate and adamant and kept on doing soaring eloquent discourses on all the details of it. What I like about you is that, on the one hand, you are giving the necessary education on the source of the evil, the cause of the evil, and hidden influences that eveyone needs to hear crystal clear about. And at the same time you are not just dwelling on that, you're also providing the solutions. You're providing the mechanisms, the formulas, the actions — civil actions, legal actions, community actions, and that's really where the direction needs to go.*

Anna, you have also news to share, whenever you feel like it, about class action lawsuits that are addressing some of these issues.

ANNA: Well, we have several things under way that are major claims in commerce, major claims in various venues in the law that I designed to bring a systemic remedy. And that's really what we want, because, basically, there are millions of people who don't have the education, don't have the will and the time, are not skilled or brave enough, nor have the money to correct this.

If you have to go through this and correct it step by step yourself doing your own due dillegence it's going to cost you, well, probably around $500 dollars, and it's going to take a lot of your time and effort to just familiarize yourself with the situation, know who you are, stand on your own two feet, and go after those rats on their own turf.

So that's just not a propsition that everybody can do and it's not a proposition that everybody *should* do in turns of, you know, exposing themselves to the court system that is in place now.

So what we're going after is a systemic remedy by which all Americans will have their baseline political status restored to them as Birthright State Nationals and all this stuff will get openly discussed and aired and people will finally understand how the government is supposed to function, how it is now functioning, and what their choices are.

Now, I'm not saying anything against the federal civilian employees. I'm not saying anything against the military service men and their families, against federal law service assistants, or political assylum seekers. Nothing. These people deserve our help and our support, and especially I am not saying anything against African Americans who were cheated, and were the first victims — along with the Native Americans — of this entire venal system that comes in after the Civil War.

We thought, "Oh! We won the Civil War! Slavery is abolished! Whee!" People turned out by the millions, celebrating. Ya. Well, it was short-lived. These European bankers came in here and in their view all the freed slaves were chattel, were possessions, and the titles to them we're up for grabs.

So what did these foreign bankers do? They put titles — they seized upon the names of these plantation slaves and did bonds and they monetized those bonds, and they used them and their property as collateral backing the debts of the United States Government Service Corporation, and, basically, what happened, was that *private* slavery was outlawed, the plantation owners could no longer own slaves — but *public* slave ownership was launched.

And if you look at the 13th Amendment which supposedly abolished slavery, you will see that it does no such thing. It abolishes slavery in one breath and then turns right around and says that criminals can be enslaved. And then in the next section, the 14th Amendment created the "criminal", which is the federal "person".

So they seized upon the titles to the freed plantation slaves, used that as collateral for the government debt, and that's where all this got started with a terrible, terrible betrayal of the American Negroes. And that is why Doctor Martin Luther King had to come forward in the 60's and demand equal civil rights.

Now, I don't know about the rest of you, how old you were when all this was happening, or not, but I was in Middle School, an early teenager at the time, when all the stuff was going on, and I remember asking myself, what's all this about civil rights? What are civil rights? Why are they different from any other kind of rights? And do all those black people *need* equal rights? And what are they equal to? And then, when you say equal rights, it implies that there is some kind of standard out there that you have to match up. Right?

Well, when you dig into this a little bit you find out that civil rights are "privileges" inferred by the government, by congress. The government gives you "civil rights" and congress can take civil rights away. And the thing that Doctor King was trying to secure, and wanted equal to, were the natural and unalienable rights of the American States National.

So, as long as there are American States Nationals, then there are no limits. The Congress has agreed to provide equal civil rights, but Congress has never been a good organization in money memory. The Congress has been a perfect organization, back to the 1860s, so instead of graciously accepting the fact that now black men and women would have rights equal to the American State Citizens, they set upon a course to undermine the actual and unalienable rights of the State Citizens too. So that they could enslave us *all,* forever.

And if you think about the way they've done this — they come to a woman whose in a hospital having just given birth, and they present her with paperwork that on the surface of it looks like it's just standard paperwork that records the birth event. That such and such a baby was born on such and such day, to such and such parents.

You have to be a legal eagle to look at that paperwork and understand what it says. And these women are not legal eagles, and they're not at their best, they're groggy, drugged up, God only know, and here they are there, signing their paperwork under conditions of non-disclosure — and what that paperwork does is, Number one, it identifies the mother as just an informant. Number two, it idenetifies the mother as an unwed mother. Number three, it gives that baby and the name of that baby, over as a Ward of the State.

This process needs to be nipped in the bud right there. All these hospitals and hospital administrators, eveybody has been thinking and saying this, and just, you know, obey the law of the State which is nothing more than a corporate franchise, like McDonalds, or Arbys, and has no more authority over you than that.

They've been doing this, and entrapping people, in this way, and seizeing control of babies and property, to be owned by the corporation as something donated to them by the mother who is never told anything about this.

When my mother found out, she was so mad that at 93 she wrote out an upteen page affidavit and took it down to the local clerk of court and filed it. Ha! And I think that everybody in America, who finds any of those actions in any hospital, now knows what to do.

Just stand back on your little fat feet and say, hey, I'm the mother of this baby, and it's a living baby, and it's a little man or woman, and its name is the name that I gave it, and now I do not intend to give it as a Ward of the State. And for a lot of us, we're not unwed mothers either.

And by the way, they're not US Citizens. They're American State Nationals. Now fix that up in your pipe and blow it.

I don't know about the rest of you, but this improbable situation has got to stop. It cannot be allowed to go on any more.

And I just became aware of this, anyway, when I had my own son. I was troubled about checking the unwed box, that I was married. And they wanted to argue about it. My husband had to come in to the hospital room and stand there and tell them that, yes, we were married. OK?

But that was only one side, and then I got to thinking about it, and I asked them why does it say I am the informant? Why doesn't it say that I am the mother? So I thought some more about it and wrote the word "mother". Right? OK? And that just about drove them appocalyptic.

Those two women coming in said you have to sign this, and if you don't sign this we're going to keep the baby here at the hospital and not let you take him home. And they had a big brawny male nurse standing in the doorway, and I'm still in my hospital bed having just given birth.

You got this scenario down? Are you beginning to get a little bit red around the ears? Are you thinking that's enough? What's going on here? Why was it so important? And why would you threaten the mother with the loss of her child, and basically kidnap the child, if she refuses to sign this piece of paper?

"As It Is The Truth!"

Well it's because the State is so damned high. It's because they're going to loose millions, and millions of dollars in property, if you don't sign that paper, and you just refuse to acquiesce and to say that you and your baby are US Citizens.

Start saying that *you are not a US Citizen.* Don't sign the paperwork. Tell them you don't have to, you're an *Amarican State National* and they can go fly their flag.

You see how vicious this is? You see how they have created an entire class of people that they're trying to enslave, even though slavery has been outlawed internationally since 1996, and yet they've created an entire class of people that are de facto slaves.

TOM: *And this is why they discourage private home births, and midwives, and that sort of thing.*

ANNA: Yes, absolutely, 100% !

TOM: *Anna, I heard about a couple that had a baby in a hospital and they just didn't give the name, and the doctor kept saying what's the name, and they said, well, we're still thinking about it. And they kept putting it off, and finally they got discharged and went home. So there was no Social Security Number assigned to the baby because they never had a name to it, to attach it to, because they named it after they got home.*

ANNA: The Name is The Mark of the Beast. And that's laid out in the Bible because Adam was given the job of naming the animals and things. So that's The Mark of the Beast, because if you have a name you're either an animal or a thing — in the Christian doctrine, anyway.

And I suspect that that is part of why and how the Church went astray, with the problem of how do you name a living baby and not get into trouble with The Mark of the Beast?

Well, I have a solution for them. I consider a name a possession, like a bicycle, or a lamp, or a chest of china. Something that you inheret. It's a station. It's yours. It's property. And it's extenal to you. So, you know, the name is a thing. You're *not* a thing. OK? And that's how we should handle this.

We should look at a name as a thing that is apart from us, a possession. A tool that we use, put on, and mainly, you know, as they've gotten desperate and tried to get out of the repercussions of what they've done, and they try to weasle around and say, "Oh no, we're not crooks", they set upon the idea that your *surname* can be seized upon by the public entity, because, after all, there are lot of "Johnsons" and there are a lot of, you know, Olsons. And most people don't know where their surname comes from.

So they seized upon this as a public asset and the Church actually says . . . the Holy See actually says that your name is your first and middle name, and that it is your property, and that's who you are in the law, and so it's the upper-lower case first and middle name, not the last at all, that represents the livng being, the living individual being.

Um. . . So that's their system. And when you use your *surname* in that system you are identifying yourself as a vessel in commerce, in the maritime commerce of admiralty. So, anyway, all this stuff is recoursing around religion and around terrible missuse of sacred trusts and law forms that have been confirmed, and bonds, and kicked around and compelled with each other, for a millenium.

But before we leave the whole topic here, I want to bring up something else that happened back in the Civil War, earlier, so that people will have an understanding of the court system that they are facing today.

What they are facing are adminstrative martial law common law courts. That's what is occupying your court houses and giving the false impression that they are public and civilian, when they're not. They are . . . There are two kinds of courts that are operating out of our court houses today and pretending to be our courts when they are not.

They're for US Citizens, and there are two kinds of US Citizens. There are living people who are US Citizens with upper and lower case names, who are living people who have been born in federal states, like someone from Puerto Rico or Guam. They really are legitimately US Citizens. And thanks to all of the obscene stuff that went on after the Civil War, African Americans are US Citizens who were never given their national status, so they are United States Citizens, upper and lower case — and then there are all these "corporate personas" that they named after us and marketed to the world for their own benefit, and those are named in all-capital-letters.

So these courts — there are two kinds. One of them is for people who are United States Citizens, and the other deals with the Corporations. Neither one of these has a damned thing to deal with you. It's completely spurious that they even have addressed you or send mail to you, in mail fraud, and send mail to you when you are NOT actually and *voluntarily* a United States Citizen.

Anyway, you have an administrative court and you have a martial common law admiralty court. And the genesis of these courts in America is rather peculiar in that it all goes back to the Civil War.

As we have said earlier, the Northern states were bankrupt and the Southern states were in ruin. And the Army was in charge under the Lieber Code. So Congress — which was not really Congress — was a thing calling itself the United States Congress, not the Federal States in Congress Assembled.

A United States Corporate Congress was in charge and they said that the military commanders could appoint people in their districts to run courts for the purpose of dealing with Rebels, and these 10 districts in the southern states, were set up so that the generals of the United States could appoint their pals to come to these southern states, instead of judges, and fleece everybody blind.

This is where the Carpet Baggers came from. All those people came down from the north to take up the slack and root and pillage and steal from the southerners. And that's what they did. They set up these quasy civil military tribunals under the guize of being civilian courts, and they're not. And they plundered them. And that's what they are still doing today. They just expanded it all over the country.

Now, there was a great cry over this back in the 1860's and there was a supreme court case that came up called "Milligan ex parte" that very clearly states that the American States Government is operating, and the people are setting up their common law courts, so there is no excuse for these other courts to be in existence, and they have to go back to their normal jurisdiction, and just be adminstrative courts for federal purposes. Right?

But because we didn't know what was going on because we were not told by the vermin, that were making the big move, their inland piracy order. These court eventually took over, and that's what we've got now. A military tribunal being run by cronies for the purpose of fleecing us.

And the way out of it is for us to honor our own obligations to be self governing, to take back our Birthright Status as American States Nationals, to hold our own elections, set up our own courts, train and educate our own federal marshals, and get of of this life.

And then we can invoke Milligan ex parte and take these private corporate tribunals and military courts right out of our court houses and they'll have to go pay their own rent.

TOM: *This is fantastic!*

ANNA: Well, when all of this stuff came up, someone said to me, "how do you know all this stuff"? I know all this stuff because Americans have been duking at different parts of this for generations. I know all this stuff because things didn't add up, you know. Ask yourself this question, which I asked at 31, in my own life, "If we're so free, why is it that we have to pay out 40% of our income? Well if we're so free why do we have to fill out this paperwork and give over 40% of our income to the government?" Hello?

If we are so free, why is it that these so called government agents think that they can trespass on our property at will? Why do they think that they can just come to our house and bang on the door and come bouncing in as some sort of — I don't know — Swatt team on steroids? Why do they think they can do that?

There are a lot of things that just did not and do not add up. And I think that a certain amount of scepticism and curiosity about such basic issues that affect yourself and so many others is absolutely necessary. I mean think of the harm that we have done by sleepily allowing this to go on. Think of all the money that we have put out in taxes and the harm and damage *we* have done by stupidly allowing this to go one.

And then think about all of the missuse of that money. Think about what Congress has done with that money in terms of harming others and profiteering and racketeering and causeing trouble in the world. It's just mind boggling, and *we* supported it. We have innocently supported it, but we supported it none-the-less.

TOM: *Anna this is a fantastic overview of both history and the current situation that's deeply insightful. It's a lot of what some people know already, somewhat and partially, but you've filled in a lot of the details, a lot of the insights that go beyond the average understanding, and we really appreciate it, and it's amusing too, because when I originally asked you about coming on the show, you said, how long will it go, and I said, you can talk as long as you want, up to 3 hours, and you said, OK, I don't think I can talk that long. And then your passion came out. But there are questions I want to ask you, if it's ok with you to go on to some of those?*

ANNA: Sure.

TOM: *There are a several websites, brillianceincommerce.com — Anna's basic site, asanbank.net — karatgroupsite.com/ ameagle1956.html — that will give you access to the gold business in Anna's network, and for those who called in and who are listening who came in through other introducers, get back with the person who introduced you for their link to Karatbar, from the person who invited you.*

And now for other people who have questions —

CALLER: *We know that you levied a $279 trillion dollar lien against the BAR Association and against all the dirty buggers. I've been studying the UCC which is their very system. But it is a system that we can beat them at. You had to become a se-cured party creditor with your UCC filings. You obviously understood what the bond is. OK. And so it was mentioned in the outline for this show that it's a non-UCC strategy that you are now working on. And we just hallow you for this, that you are working on, and for your insights. If you could address this question, I would appreciate it.*

ANNA: First and foremost, commerce is not my strongest suit. I can move my head around in it the . . .

In my prayers at night, I see a world where nobody has to maneuver around in commerce or answer to admiralty courts about anything. That's my goal. So the leins were Judge Steve Curry's brainchild, and I signed on the leins because I didn't want him to be standing there alone.

He was brave enough to do it but I didn't want him standing there with nobody else backing him up. So that's why I signed on that lien, and the lien has now even been perfected. And my unserstanding is that the intention is to monetize the lien.

A lien is a security interest, as you all know, and so we have a perfected $279 trillion dollar lien against the AMERICAN BAR ASSOCIATION and the INTERNATIONAL BAR ASSOCIATION and their members. You can take that to a bank and the bank can monetize that for you based on the debts that are owed.

Now at the time this was done the BAR ASSOCIATION was feeling very cocky about this, that they could deal with the rubes and they wouldn't face any consequences. They were so arrogant that they didn't bother to even respond to Judge Curry's lien. However, the world of commerce is nothing if not draconian. If you ignore that kind of a presentment you do so at your own risk, and we have since learned all of the processes necessary to enforce that lien in court.

So I think that the lawyers that have been so eager to have been BAR ASSOCIATION members, who have clung to their BAR cards and let the BAR ASSOCIATION rule them, are going to be very eagerly tearing up those same BAR cards and coming back to operating as "lawyers" instead of "attorneys", and foreswearing any foreign titles and emoluments and actually getting back to an honest practice of law, instead of the kind of scullduggery that they've been involved it.

So anyway, I would suspect that if I were facing a $279 trillion dollar lien, I would pretty much call that organization's bond, because sooner or later half of their members are going to be taking enough hits, that they're not going to be in business. And that was the actual intention of the lien, to put the BAR ASSOCIATIONS out of business, which is to out and out bankrupt them.

And I hope that answers your question.

TOM: *OK. Thank you very kindly. Next we have another question.*

CALLER: *My question is for Judge Anna. Looking at the Federal Reserve note status, or where it presently is in our* *economy, where to you see that five years from now, and will companies like Karatbar, or a company like Karatbar . . . how fundamental is the corporation Karatbar, with what needs to be accomplished to stabilize our country, or the economy of our planet?*

ANNA: Well, some people have almost a religious fervor about gold and understand it in ways that I don't, or at least I don't as yet. I looked at it in a very plodding practical way, that over half or the world's people are now trading in gold, China, India, Brazil, South Africa, all of Europe are basically committed to trading in gold. And all at once I think 90% of American don't have any gold at all. Now that just strikes me as being an untenable position to be in.

And so I looked at Karatbars back in 2011 which was pretty near the start of the compnay, and frankly I was turned off at that time because I just bascally don't like multi-level marketing schemes, and even though Karatbars is not a typical multi-level marketing program, it does not require you to have any on-going minimum production, or to get a certain number of people involved, or any of that kind of stuff. It just offers a percentage as commissions.

So it's not like Shakely, or some of the other things that really went to the top with multi-level marketing schemes. But I don't like those, so I was turned off.

The other thing is that even though the karatbar idea, of the little card with the small amount of gold, is appealing, as very ready and cash-like, at the time I didn't think that the 30% value of the packaging and the assaying and cutting things into small pieces really made much sense.

I wasn't seeing far enough, basically. But here's the situation. Now everybody's trading in gold, and there's going to be a forseeable increase in the amount of trading that goes on in gold and as that happens the price of gold is going to go up. Nobody knows how far but we know that it is going to go up. And as it does, that one ounce coin that you can purchase for $1300 dollars today might eventually be worth as much as $10,000 dollars. OK?

So imagine taking $10,000 dollars into the local grocery store to buy a couple of loaves of bread and some milk. It's just not practical. Things have gotten too crazy now. But Karatbars offer the advantage that they're in very small denominations, and you can take a gram of gold in and trade it. If you've got something that has gold in it at a proven quality and a proven amount, you can use it as cash and nobody is going to be standing there wondering about it what it is, and that can be a life saver. And the other thing is that Karatbar has initiated a program where you can have potentially a Master Card or a Debit Card that is based on your gold holdings and your commissions if you have them that allows you to have a credit card that works.

So that even if the fiat system and the fiat currency goes completely cofluey, you'll still have a credit card that works. And that can be a life saver too. And especially for mom and pop.

People who can invest in bullion and buy it by the bar are not the people I'm worried about. It's the little guy who has to make the rent, and live life and feed the family, that I'm worried about. And even though Karatbar does have a significant cost attached to its packaging, and the label that goes into assaying and cutting the gold up into small portions, it does offer significant advantages to mom and pop.

You can buy gold in these small quantities much more affordably than you have to buy a whole one once coin of it. A lot of the people who I am concerned about don't have an extra $1300 dollars in their back pocket to spend on a one once Krugerrand or something like that.

Ya . . . Well, I'm glad everybody is out there listening. It's very important. So are there any more questions?

TOM: *We don't need a currency to . . . it's kind of like a mechanism. It works when you have gold or silver backing but there are people who've done great work like Steven Salinga, at Monetary.org, or the American Monetary Institute, as well as Bill Still, at Money Masters.com. They've written a bill that would fix the monetary system tomorrow, but until the people become aware of this, then it will finally happen, but Ezra Pound was the one who summed all this up in a nutshell. He said, "The scourge of today is the ignorance of the monetary systems, like the scourge of previous centuries was inability to read plain print."*

ANNA: Well, that's true and it's also untrue, because most people are not trained to read legalese. I am aware of the technical meanings of terms that are imbeded in them, you know, like in pieces of legislation that is hidden away, and there's really no reason why they should be.

When you are dealing with the public, you should be dealing with them *as* the public. And you should take into your scheme of things, that people don't know legal jargon, and they shouldn't be expected to. And they shouldn't be taken advantage of because they don't. And the principle of fair play and honesty should protect and pertain even more to those who do not have advanced education.

We need to have a benevolent and kind, and compassionate attitude to the other people in this world. And that includes the people who have a *good* education, who have had the opportunity to advance themselves, and have professions, to be in responsible positions — to honor what society has made possible for them and to honor it by protecting and defending those who are less fortunate who are not educated and can't do it for themselves, instead of preying upon them.

What kind of world is it when those who have received the lion share of the best of things turn around and grind their heels into the poor, and make fun of them, and call them livestock, and strut around in their fancy designer clothes, and do all of these evil things.

That is so totally wrong. That is the opposite of what should be happening. Those who have been given the experience should be right here demanding change. They're the ones who should be here going, Uh, Uh. No, Mr Congressman, that isn't going to happen that way. They're the ones who should be taking these judges to task.

You know, my great aunt Sally shouldn't have to have a law degree to go downtown and buy a car without getting fleeced senseless, you know. I'm sorry. My neighbor should not have to pay a mortgage when he's already paid that mortgage and far more, the moment he left the closing table.

And none of us should have to have a law degree and have searched through the Congressional record of 1863 to know what "personal" means so that we can avoid entrapment at the bank. These are things that people, like me have to go off and fight.

And it may be an odd circumstance that I'm a grandmother, a great grand monther, in Big Lake Alaska, but I'm not going to stand here and put up with it. Not for me. Not for my fanily. Not for my neighbors. Not for my friends, Not even for my enemies. I am hoping that everybody feels the same way, and that there are those who have good educations who will stand up for those who don't.

TOM: *Absolutely. You have a higher level of awareness, Anna. And those who are becoming more benevolent, those who are becoming more unwilling to accept the crimes against humanity, and who are using their intelligence to catch the criminals, to stop them in their tracks, and to administer justice, and to replace corruption with honesty, with fairness, and with generosity, and those of higher consciousness, in the future our educational system around the world will show that the greatest people in the world are those who have developed their hearts, those who have developed the capacity to care,* *their capacity to be concerned about the welfare of their neighbors, as one is about themselves.*

And it's not just following some religious rule or dial, but rather it is the extrinsic existential reality of nature and of universal law and natural law, and that what you send out comes back to you. How you treat others is a vibration, in physics, cause and effect, action reaction, where the vibrations you send out come back to you. As you sow, you reap, the law of Karma, or whatever you want to call it, is an operating law throughout the universe, and the universe is governed by that.

Humans have and are realizing that we're not here to exploit and to dominate, and to enslave, and to harm others, and it's not necessary, either, to be happy or to be prosperous. It's not necessary to harm any life anywhere in order for one's own happiness, satisfaction and success to devlope. On the contrary, one's own success is greater if one is willing to be of assistance and service to others.

So that's the basis upon which the new system is unfolding, and that's why everyone loves you, Anna, and loves eveyone who is aligning themselves with these principles.

ANNA: Well, you know . . . I use to be a coward. Up until about the 3rd grade. When I was in the 3rd grade, one afternoon after school, this 6th grader named . . . well I won't name him . . . he beat up my best fried. She was in the 3rd grade with me and he way-laid her after school and he just tossed her into a snowbank and was kicking her and she was there helpless . . . and I lost it! I absolutely became a human buzz saw. I lost my cowardness at that moment.

And there is some stuff of which I will not put up. And I'm not going to stand here and watch millions of Americans be mistreated and mischaracterized and defrauded by people that are taking their paycheck from my pocket. It's not going to happen on my watch. I'm sorry.

I don't give a good gofloowy what the generals think, or what they don't like, or what Mr. Putin thinks, of how Pope Francis feels about it. I'm not going to put up with it. And I encourage all of you to put your hands up and say no I'm not going to put up with it either.

I'm and American States National. I was born in California.

TOM: *So we have a number of callers who have questions. We also have our other guest, Royal, here available. We don't have any limit to how long we can talk and it's entirely up to you. What would you like to proceed with, Anna?*

ANNA: Well, I just want to give credit to Patrick Devine and Mark Emery and to their group. There has been some real significant movement that I think is powerful and potentially great ways for people to resolve all kind of debts, and to help their country to put an end to the abuses that are going on. But in order to answer your questions appropriately, I have to go into more detail. It goes back to the Name.

When you were born you were given a Name. Let's pretend that your name is "Linda Anne George". That name would be written in upper and lower case, and that's how you grew up in grade scool, and that's how you were taught to write your name on all of your school work. And that's the name you used your whole life long.

But you have also received a lot of different kinds of bills over the years addressed to LINDA ANNE GEORGE in all capital letters. OK? And recently you have also begun receiving letters addressed to LINDA A GEORGE, with just your middle initial, and all in capital letters.

Now when you see something in all capital letters that is your clue that the only thing that that can be is a dead man's estate or a corporation. So essentially what they've done is FDR used to sign your upper and lower case name and made it a surety of the bankruptcy of the American corporation known as the United States of America, Inc. back in 1933. So that vessel in commerce was out of commission and in control of the bankruptcy trustees until 1999.

So all those years that you were using that name prior to 1999 it wasn't in your control, it was in control of the bankruptcy trustees that were intent on getting money out of you for creditors.

In 1999 that whole bankruptcy that you were unknowingly and unwillingly a part of, ended. And your name, your upper and lower case name was discharged, and you received it back free and clear. But you have not gone forth and straightened things our to take back that name now that's it's free and clear, and make it your own, and under your control. OK?

So you need to do an adult name change. Right now they've got you as LINDA ANN GEORGE in all caps. That's the name that was in their system for you. And as a first step in taking back control of who you are, you need a Name. One that you can control, and that is on the record as your name, belonging to you, as your possession.

And you need a name that is free and clear of debt. So you go and change your name back from upper case, to upper and lower case, and that way you gain control of an international vessel, a trade name that you can take using to trade or to deal in commerce, or whatever you want, because it's a sovereign name again. OK?

So you reclaim what was yours. You reclaim your original name by doing a name change back from the all upper case, to upper and lower case name. Then what you do is you expatriate that name from any assumption of any US Citizenship at all. And there are two kinds of US Citizens, like I was explaining, so you want to specifically say that *"I willingly and of my own free act expatriate from any assumption of US Citizenship, and from United Sates Citizenship, or being a citizen of the United States, which is a corporate person. And I herewith insist and grant allegience to the soil of Virginia where I was born."*

You take it back to the land, you take it back to the actual soil which is your inheritance as one of the People who lives here, and you leave it at that.

Now what you're done, is you have captured a trust and a vessel that you can use, it's your possession, it's your property, it's your name, officially now on the court record, and you have dry-docked that vessel in it's permanent port home which is Virginia, or California. It's where your soil is, it's where you live, where you were born, or where you are going to be. OK?

So go back to the dry land as your point of origin. So now you are outside of their clutches. You're operating totally within your realm. You are in charge of your name and your vessel and your property that you situated and claimed back to the land of your birthright, or to where you are living.

Now the next thing is, that you still have these other two names out there tooling around causing trouble. Right? Those things are still being traded on the stock market. Those things are still US Citizens and you don't really have control of those names because those were created by other parties after the fact based upon your birth name and you are the priority creditor of those names, but they don't really belong to you, and in fact, each one of those names represents an entire series of legal constructs, called legal fiction entities.

The first one, the all capital letter name LINDA ANN GEORGE is a Centui Que Trust. That is, a form of trust that is created when somebody is lost and missing at sea, or lost in a dissaster like a fire, or a volcano, or something of that sort, where it's not known if they're alive or dead.

So the state comes in and claims the Centui Que Trust that's named after that individual person. All right?

So now you've got the Centui Que Trust. Well, who was missing?

Ah. You're upper and lower case name was missing. Right? OK. So you've got to get control of those two other names. And they don't belong to you, so how are you going to do that?

Well, you've got two choices. You can do it through probate, or you can do it through bankruptcy. And I have gone round and round, and round and round about this.

What's the best way to collapse these things? Of course, probate the estate without harming the living man or woman. And there are some advantages of probate. But if you've changed you name to the upper and lower case form, you're in a good position. You have your trust established, you have your vessel established, and you have your point of origin established, and your domicile established, and now you're in a position where you can do a third party forced liquidation of those two entities, and one of the things that Patrick's group found out is that the proper, technical way of looking at this is that these are organizations and they give some very good information abour how to proceed on how to do a non-UCC claim, and how to then record that claim and proceed through the Chapter 7 Bankruptcy and force them to do away with their bogus false personas and disharge all your debts, your mortgages, college loans, car loans, house loans, credit card loans, all that stuff, and leave you with a big significant nest egg to go forward into the future. And all of that info is being discussed right now at the lighthouseliberty.club.

Now, they have a wonderful U-Tube presentation on U-Tube. It's called "Settle All Debts" or "Settle All Claims", that's it, and I would recomment that you go there and listen carefully to that and run it through a couple of time to get it straight in you head and then join the Law Club and go on their blog and their forums and start talking to people who are also involved in that and start gathering this information, and gathering the forms that you will need, and getting familiar with the process.

It's a little bit of work. I'm not going to joke. It's probably going to take you, I don't know, probably 8 hours at least to familiarize yourself with the whole thing. And then probably another 10 hours to gather up all the different documents. So you're looking at a little piece of work, and you're probably looking at, well in Alaska it's $106 dollars to file a Chapter 7 Bankruptcy, and I think it's something in that neighborhood in all other states.

This is an unusual Chapter 7 Bankruptcy because most Chapter 7 Bankruptcies are people that are so deep in debt that they just can't make it anymore, so they file bankruptcy to escape their own debt.

But this is a diffent kind of animal. It's a third party forced liquidation by the priority creditor against these two organizations. The bankrupt US Citizenship Organization and the bankrupt US Public Utility Transmitting Organization which is what that other name with just the middle initial is a public transmitting utility of which is bankrupt.

You have to go after both of them in order to get debt-clear. Anyway, that information is there and I would just get involved and get going.

TOM: *OK. Well, thank you very much. Thank you so much. Anna, you could found a University, and maybe you will. So we are just beyond our 3 hour limit but we're still on the line. This is fabulous, absolutely fabulous, and we're very very grateful. We're going to have you on again in the future for sure to continue. There will be much much more news to share as we proceed.*

*So everyone, once again, the websites are **www.brilliance-incommerce.com**, and then Anna, you were sharing the **www.lighthouseliberty.club** by Mark Emery. Mark Emery is a freedom guy. He has fought his own battles with the IRS and won them.*

ANNA: And, I guess I got his Irish up and he's been nibbling away on them too. Yes, Lighthouse Libery Club is a real fine little membership organization at $25 dollars a month, and believe me that's nothing compaired with the information that they are working on, and what they share, and just the overall spirit of the people that are there, and I highly recommend them.

I know that there are 6 million people out there in the process of loosing their homes through foreclosure, or have recently lost their homes to bogus forclosures, and, yes, they cry out to me, and want me to help them, but there just isn't anyway that I can. There just isn't enough time in anyones's life to even begin scrapping 6 million mortgage foreclosure cases, but the www.lighthouseliberty.club has come up with an answer which, in addtion to the name change which does away with some other problems, should work very very well, and should be very difficult for the fraudsters to overcome. And it has the potential of not only settling the foreclosures, but settling all the other debts and problems people have, actually giving them back some benefit from all that they suffered as a result of the abuse and fraud that's been practiced against them.

TOM: *And everyone, for unsecured debts, we've been 100% successful with those as well in the United States. So that is available for those who have a credit card or student loan debt, and need relief from those. So we have a lot of solutions, a lot of remedies, a lot of opportunities to gain a lot of knowledge and more to come, and more future episodes.*

Anna, we thank you. You're a beautiful being. We'd like to have you back. Let's continue as we have time, and may you be healthy and successfull and happy, and continue to live a few more thousand years at least, if you wish, on this plane.

ANNA: OK.

TOM: *Well thank you. And take care. And Royal, we thank you very kindly for your contribution, and we look forward to having you on again in the future as well. Every one. Enjoy. Have a wonderful Day. And let's reconvene. OK? Bye, Bye.*

"As It Is The Truth!"

*"Take heed that no man deceive you.
For many shall come in my name, and shall deceive
many."— Matthew 24:4,5.*

If you really are serious about knowing how to restore the Republic and your freedom you need to put some effort into knowing how our freedoms are being robbed from us by fraud, lack of full disclosure, deception, threat, duress, coercion, and intimidation every day of our lives and have been for over 100 years by the criminals who have hijacked our government, wealth, and heritage for their own gain and evil intentions.

Listen to this interview with Judge Anna while you read transcript:

Judge Anna Riezinger - 02-20-2016 RBN (in Defence of Humanity) source : **https://www.youtube.com/watch?v=lhFmhqG-ARw**

3

Interview with Judge Anna Von Reitz

HOSTESS: *Please read and enjoy the In Defense of Humanity page listed at the top of the AntiCorruption Society home page.*

Normally I co-host this program with Ingry Cassel of **vaclib.org** *however Ingry is off tonight. So tonight I've invited a guest, a wonderful guest to join us. She is on the line but I'd like to introduce her a little bit before I bring her on.*

I just first found out about this wonderful researcher and grandmother with a heart of gold, back in 2014 when I read an article she wrote called, "Where The Bear Went, And Where We Are". I was absolutely astounded, I mean it basically started with a letter which she had written to the Arch Bishop of Chicago, and who essentially called him on the carpet and got the American People off the hook because somehow in his communication he felt that what was going wrong with America was the fault of the voters -- the electorate.

And Anna just explained beautifully how the American people are not at fault for what has happened to us. We say that on this show all the time.

The American people did not choose to be in the pickle we're in. This was all done by stealth and Anna has written about it over and over again exposing the fraud that has gone on since before we were all born.

So I have on our webpage an article that I just posted today called Judge Anna von Reitz, On In Defense of Humanity, and I gave a little bit of Introduction how she has spent decades researching both the history of our country and the devolution of our legal system.

Anna was a major contributer to the filing of a lien against the American BAR Association, the International BAR Association, and the Department of Justice. We have a link to that on that page on that article.

Anna's discoveries regarding the IRS are absolutely mind blowing, and what really got my attention was her explanation of the ongoing crime that she calls "personage". It was brilliant and it is so apropos to what we talk about on this program and what is going on every day across the country.

Anna . . . you can tell that I'm impressed with what you have done. Are you there?

ANNA: Yes, I'm here.

HOSTESS: *Great, I'm so glad you're on.*

ANNA: Well, I'm pleased to be here.

HOSTESS: *Yes. You've been extremely brave to process the paperwork that you've been processing. Like a lien against the American BAR Association. That was wonderful. I mean, it was long overdue. I'm also glad you did it.*

ANNA: Well, I can't take a whole lot of credit for that. My expertise is not commercial law. I'm kind of a neophyte in terms of commercial law. The lien was actually written by Judge Steve Curry of Colorado and he has that particular expertise, and the rest of us signed on to basically protect him and to stand up for what we believe to be the truth.

So I was kind of a follower more than a leader in that effort, but now Steve has been attacked and thrown in jail under false arrest, that was several months ago. And what it was, he caught some of the local government officials and others involved in selling just plain old rocks as meteorites.

So he called them on it, and he was brought into court, charged falsely on the part of corrupt local officials, and he was charged by their corporate court with a year of community service for his supposed crime of objecting to their criminality, and he did not serve that year of community service so they charged him with a parole violation and brought him back in and they have him in jail for this ridiculous situation right now. It's crazy.

But anyway. He has been in the same situation that we've all been in, in that we've all been operating under one set of assumptions, and behind our back a whole other set of assumptions have been put in place. We've all been misrepresented. We've all had our identity stolen, and we've all been removed from our natural birthright Jurisdiction on the Land, to the foreign International Jurisdiction of the Sea. And our estates have been held in "abeyance" under International Law, but that then has allowed members of the BAR to come in, and acting in sedition against our lawful government and against us, has allowed us to be plundered and pillaged under the laws of international commerce.

So here we are thinking that we are protected under the Constitution and that we have certain guarantees.

But the Constitution is the Law of the Land. Why should you incorporate anything? Including the franchise of a corporation merely named after you, which is what they've done. They can then pretend that you are the same as the corporation which is the crime of "personage".

And they can bring false claims against that person, which is another crime known a "barratry", named after the BAR Associations. So they've been committing this crime against us, creating these "persons" without our knowledge and consent, and that is the "person" being charged in every single court case that you can bring before me. There are only a limited number of these "persons" out there so they're trying to create more all the time, and every single court case that I have ever examined, which is many many thousands of court cases by now, have been against a "person", not a living people -- not a member of living people.

So this is what they're doing. They're using these two crimes, and basically identity theft. They're kidnapping us and our assets, and our land assets, into the international jurisdiction of the Sea, which is a crime known as "press-ganging".

Your history buff friends will be reminded that during the Napoleon Wars, the Queen had need for more people to operate Her Majesties Navy, so the British Ship of War would come into a quiet hamlet, and then sailors would go ashore and they would grab any able bodied man that they could find and they would "press-gang" him into service in the navy. So all of these farmers were being kidnapped to work ships on the Sea.

Well, this was finally outlawed, and its been outlawed now for almost 200 years, and yet they're doing it today. So it's kidnapping and "press-ganging" on the high seas, and then they are additionally plundering our assets of the land, our homes, our businesses, our land assets -- everything, which is "inland piracy". Another capital crime.

And just today I was going over the Nuremburg Trial Principles. They've violated all seven. OK? This could not possibly be a more serious crime. It's both a commercial crime and a war crime against defenseless non-combatant civilians. And this has been done to us by foreign governments and by international banks. And I want everyone to know that the principle banks responsible for this are the Federal Reserve, the World Bank, and the International Bank of Reconstruction and Development, and the International Monetary Fund. These four banks are the principle conspirators, and they have acted in collusion with each other to front governmental services corporations.

Now, under the Constitution, the federal government was given certain duties, certain functions to perform which are called

"As It Is The Truth!"

"powers", but which should more correctly in modern terms be called "abilities" or "services" to perform. Those 19 enumerated "services" are all in international jurisdiction. There isn't a single one of them that has anything legitimately to do with the land or the people on the land. Our government was set up so that there was this strict demarkation to make sure that the federal government did not usurp upon us.

Now what happened here is that there is not a functioning federal government. There is in fact just a governmental services corporation providing these 19 central governmental services, as presumed successors to contract.

Let me give you an example of this. And this is very close to the truth of what is going on here. Say that I were to hire a lawn maintenance company, mom and pop lawn maintenance company to come in and mow my lawn, and rake my leaves, and fertilize my grass, and water it during dry spells, and do all these associated tasks.

And then that mom and pop business is forced into bankruptcy. It's no longer able to do the job, for whatever reasons. So, another company comes in and starts doing all of those jobs, at the same price and everything, as the original company, and I don't say anything about this. I don't even know that there's been a change in uniform or truck that has come onto my property to do these things. They're all just getting done, I'm paying a bill, and the bill may come to me as a GCB Corporation instead of ABC Company, but I'm kind of a typical average person, and I don't notice that there's been any big change. I just assume that everything's all right. My lawn is getting taken care of.

That's a "successor to contract" in commerce.

When you don't question that kind of a change-over, then that company or corporation that took over can operate on the presumption that they have inherited the contract. OK?

Now if I stood up and said right away, "Hey wait a minute, who are you? I have a contract with ABC Company and you're GCB Corporation. I don't have a contract with you." Well, then you're going to have to renegotiate and have a new contract, or not. But if you don't do that, they can just assume that they are the successor, and that they have a contract with you.

Now this is what was done to us as the entire country as a nation.

I want you to put yourself back to the end of the Civil War, and where are we, now.

Well, we have eleven States in the south that are under military occupation, and all of the Northern States are bankrupt. There is nobody in control of this entire continent except the Grand Army of the Republic, the Union Army, and a Corporation operating as THE UNITED STATES OF AMERICA in Washington, D.C. which is using the remaining members of Congress -- the old Congress that was elected in 1860 -- as a Board of Directors. Now what did I say before? If you take anything and you incorporate it, you take it off the Land, straight into the international Jurisdiction of the Sea.

So what's going on here at the end of the Civil War? Well, we've got a Military that is operating under General Order 100, the Lieber Code, which Abraham Lincoln adopted and enforced upon his Generals just prior to declaring the bankruptcy of the original United States Company -- the United States trading Company that had been providing governmental services, and you have the Congress operating as The United States of America, Incorporated, a Delaware Corporation. OK?

That's what you've got at the end of the Civil War. There is no actual what we would call a lawful government. There's just a Military enforcing its rules and its Lieber Code instructions, and a commercial corporation that is endeavoring to provide the essential governmental services, as a successor to contract. All right? See all that?

HOSTESS: *How did the Carpetbaggers fit into that?*

ANNA: The Carpetbaggers were Northerners who came to the South, and basically they we're doing then what they're doing now, OK, right after Lee's Army surrendered at Appomattox. Right?

Well, we are taught that that's the end of the Civil War, but in point of fact, that was just the surrender of Lee's Army to Grant's Army. It was an "Armistice," it was not a peace treaty. In fact, there is no peace treaty that ended the Civil War.

PROGRAM BREAK:

ANNA: Our Federal government exited stage left, incorporated, and started functioning as the commercial corporation in the governmental services business and functioning in the international Jurisdiction of the Sea as a corporation.

Well, that in itself is legal enough to do, but they then also acted as successor to contract to the original unincorporated federal services company, and that altered the nature of the services company.

It went from being a services Company on the Land, to being a services Corporation on the Sea, and there was no public understanding or description of any of this. It was just handled as an internal corporate or company business issue. And as a result the American People were never really told that his had any wide ranging implication as to how their government in those areas was being administered, and by whom?

Because when you elect members to the Congress that we know of as the United States in Congress Assembled, the people who attend that Congress are representatives of the Land Jurisdiction and they are fiduciary deputies who are 100% commercially and individually, as people, liable for what they do.

If they do do anything wrong, sneaky or bad, they can be charged, and they can loose everything they have and they can go to jail.

By Judge Anna von Reitz 79

They can even be held for Treason if they knowingly do something that undermines the welfare of the individual States that they represent, or the people they represent.

However, when you go into the international Jurisdiction of the Sea, the members of the Congress are operating as The United States Congress, not the United States in Congress Assembled, and the people attending there are just corporate officers, they're private corporate officers that have been elected to serve on a Board of Trustees for a governmental services corporation. They have no such public office, they have no such fiduciary responsibility or account-ability. They can represent you just the way an actor might represent you on a stage.

They have no public office. There is no public Oath. In fact if you go look it up you'll see that all the members of Congress are taking their Oath to the "United States", not to the "United States of America". So this has been a big semantic deceit game, and a big fraud game, and con game for a long, long time.

Now, getting back to what went on in the South after the Civil War, and with the Carpetbaggers.

Immediately after Grant accepted the surrender of Lee at Appomattox, there was considerable chaos to be dealt with, and the only force that was in place that could maintain the peace was the Grand Army of the Republic, Grant's Union Army. And the Congress was put into place even though they were just operating as a governmental service corporation. They were put into place and they went from an "enabling" clause to an "enactment" clause — an act.

PROGRAM BREAK:

ANNA: Now we're back at the end of the Civil War, and the question is about the Carpetbaggers and what went on there. Lee's Army has surrendered to Grant, there is no peace treaty, the

Congress is operating as a Board of Directors of a governmental services corporation to provide essential governmental services. The Congress, in order to provide those essential governmental services and to keep the peace in the Southern States, where all of the courts had ceased functioning, ordered the Military District Commanders to appoint civilians to act as judges operating what are called civil tribunals, but which are in fact Military Common Law Tribunals. And these civilians of course had to be Union sympathizers or actual people from the North who were brought in to act as judges and jury, and legislature, and all the rest.

The Carpetbaggers were people from the North who occupied these positions. OK?

So because they were from the North and because for the most part they were vengeful, they used these positions -- these seeming public offices -- which were military offices -- to plunder and pillage the Southerners, whether they were Union sympathizers, or rebels, or whatever.

And the instructions given by Congress were to deal with the Rebels -- the remaining Rebels in the Southern States. So this international law form, military common law, was imposed on the civilian population and this has been called by various euphemistic names, Special Admiralty, Executive Admiralty, and this is the source of the gold-fringe that you see on the flag displayed in all the court houses.

Where ever you see that war flag with the gold fringe on it, they're operating a military tribunal under military common law which gives them a very free hand to dispose of any property, to jail any people who they feel are a threat, and generally abuse the public trust, which they've been doing for generations.

So this was the form of law that they have used as a club over our heads.

However, in 1866 there was an action objecting to this, in the US

Supreme Court, and the US Supreme Court, in Milligan ex parte, handed down a decision which basically said that where ever the American common law courts are operating, it is unconscionable and unnecessary for there to be any formal military law exercised, and any such court must shut down.

So as you can see, these kinds of courts are very abusive and they are very profitable because they can be used to seize property, and take things away from people, be it land, homes, businesses, freedoms, and do whatever they want. So all these military courts can be used for these evil offices.

Now, we have the answer in our hands, in that we can turn around and reopen our American common law courts, and force them to shut down, which is why we have put such an emphasis on restoring our county governments and getting our American common law courts up and running.

When we get our American common law courts at the county level up and running, we can force them to shut down their admiralty courts at the county level. And when we get our common law state courts up an running, we can force them to shut down their federal state courts, which are also operating as military tribunals. And this is why it's so important for people to understand the situation with regard to their lawful government.

Remember what I said? When you incorporate anything, it goes -- zoom -- right out into the international Jurisdiction of the Sea. It is no longer operating under the Law of the Land.

HOSTESS: *Does that include non-profit corporations?*

ANNA: Yup. Any kind of corporation. Churches. Everything. OK?

So, all these corporations are all 100% operating under the international Law of the Sea. And so, where the federal corporation that's providing essential governmental services at the federal level, is operating in the international Jurisdiction of the Sea and using international martial common law to basically control and abuse the people of this country.

They could only do that at the federal level, initially, because the state courts, where state courts existed, were still on the land, and the county courts were still on the land, but in 1965 federal corporations had been so sucessful at its racketeering at the federal level that it was able to bribe the states and the counties into incorporating as franchises of the federal corporation in order to receive federal revenue sharing, that is, kickbacks, from federal racketeering. OK?

So, about 1965 the last of the states and counties incorporated, and when they incorporated they what? They went -- zoom -- right into the international Jurisdiction of the Sea. And this happened very very quietly. Nobody told you. Nobody announced it. And for the most part, nobody but the lawyers knew that there was any change implied.

You know, Joe Shmo was in office as the Mayor, and Joe Shmo was still Mayor the next day. The county sheriff's office was still there, and the sheriff was still the sheriff. There was no outward sign that really told any one, that -- Hey! -- we've left the Jurisdiction of the Land behind and the law of the land, and we're no longer protected by the Constitution, and this is a problem!

Nobody said that. And for the most part nobody knew it but the lawyers.

So anyway, here we are in 1965, the last of the states and the counties are incorporated, and for a time -- the most crucial offices other than the offices of judges -- come down to the sheriffs. We elect a county sheriff in good faith and on the presumption that he's there to keep the peace and enforce the law of the land, the Constitution, the public laws that we all rely upon -- right? -- but when the counties incorporated his job changed. He is no longer responsible for enforcing the organic laws which are the Constitution, the Articles of Confederation, the Declaration of Independence, the Northwest Ordinnce, the land Act of 1785, those things he's not responsible for enforcing, anymore.

He's not responsible for enforcing the public's US Statutes at Large any more. He is now being tasked to be a code and regulation and statute enforcer. So he went from being a "peace-keeping officer on the land," to being a "code enforcement officer on the sea". And code enforcement is simply the internal administrative law of the corporation. So his office went from being a "public office", to being a "private corporarate office" the same way the the offices of congress went from being "public offices" to being "private corporate offices".

OK?

So then for a long time they continued to enforce the public organic law, and the US Statutes at large as part of their job, because they were used to doing that. Right? But they were also tasked with enforcing all these corporate statutes and regulations and codes. OK? And as time went on, this became a function, because no man can serve two Masters.

It's not really a tenable situation to have a man whose job description is code enforcement officer for a corporation, to also be working a public office as a sheriff on the land enforcing the Constitution and the other public US Statutes at large, public law. Many of these men who were sheriffs at that time -- in the 60's, 70's, 80's -- struggled along endeavoring to do both jobs. One, as a voluntary function, and the other as the actual job description.

And this led to Sheriff Richard Mack and another sheriff named Prinz bringing suit all the way to the US Supreme Court because they were getting flack from the corporate managers saying that they could not enforce the Constitution, so they went all the way to the US Supreme Court, and the Supreme Court came back in *Mack &*

Prinz vs. U.S.A. Inc. saying that, yes, they *could* enforce the Constitution and other organic laws, but here's the thing, they can, they're enabled to, but will they?

And among those men who do, many of them get blackballed by the corporate interests that want a free hand to do whatever they want to do to the rest of us, and they also suffer a lot or discrimination on the job. They don't get the perks; they don't get the bonuses, they're not part of the "crew". OK? So the men that struggle along and try to do the right thing voluntarily, and take on the extra job of enforcing both the public law and the organic law of this country really take it in the shorts for being the good guy. Even though they are enabled to, and even though the Supreme Court agrees that they are enabled to.

So, the key office here, is Sheriff on the Land which has been converted to Sheriff on the Sea, from peace keeping officer to code enforcement officer. And what we need to do is get our . . . .

Well OK. I should also explain that in 1976 the Congress operating as a Board of Directors of the United States Inc., formally released all state law and all state offices to the United Nations. This outrageous action took place *via two Acts* -- note that word, Acts -- of Congress -- as in play acting -- they formalized this as the Foreign Sovereign Immunities Act (FSIA) 1976, and the International Organizations Immunities Act (IOIA).

What this means is that they acknowledged the fact that all of our public offices were [and are] vacant. They were vacated by the very act of the Counties and the States incorporating as franchises of the United States, Incorporated. OK?

So, as of 1976 they stood up and said, OK, all of these offices are vacated, they're not our responsibility anymore, we turned them over to the United Nations for safe keeping. And they never told us a word. There was no public announcement. It was just handled as a private business issue. All Right?

So, all of our public offices are vacant. We still have public offices, but they're vacated. So, when you go and elect a sheriff, you think he's going to keep the peace, and act in your behalf, and to guarantee your constitutional rights, when instead you've elected a sheriff in a private corporation to act as a private code enforcer for that corporation. And you're paying for this.

So, either you've got rocks in your head, or you need to start doing what needs to be done which is to fill those vacant public offices with people who are actually sworn as public officials and who have both the accountability and the right and responsibility to exercise those public offices and to bring order and to bring justice back to the American people.

HOSTESS: *Well, let me tell you just a little piece of what I discovered in my county that absolutely supports what you're saying. In my county they can apply for a grant from the DOT from the DHS. So we discovered that they took this grant money, signed a grant contract — somebody did, it wasn't the people — and now the terms and conditions of these grant contracts, they have brought in all kinds of new corporate rules, and we ran into one county deputy, and my husband asked him why he was stopping this car and he said that "When we are going to stop a car, before we approach the car, we are obligated to notify the Department of Homeland Security."*

ANNA: Yah. They always start with corporation rules, it's all code regulations and private statutes.

HOSTESS: *Most people are afreid to tell the truth about what the BAR has done.*

ANNA: Well, the BAR is guilty on many counts. And so is the American BAR Association. But they are more like foot-soldiers. The Banks are the real source of the problem. And their manipulation of currency is the root of the whole issue. Their greed, their profit-seeking.

"As It Is The Truth!"

Their mindless devotion to evil is what has created this entire mess.

You can take it all back 100% to the banks, and from there you can distribute the blame to the lawyers, and next you can also distribute blame to the politicians. And at each level, the blame gets more dilute. The Banks started it, the lawyers carried forward on it to profit themselves, and the politicians are kind of split into two groups. Those who are too clueless to be useful to do anything about it, and those who are corrupt. So that's kind of how all this sorts out.

HOSTESS: *The thing about the BAR, though, Anna, is that when you confront them, and I have done so at a meeting — that my city is a corporation, and you cannot be a representative government and a for-profit corporation at the same time; they are in conflict with one another. But everytime I bring it up, the lawyers just jump up and down and say that that's unimportant, we're not going to talk about that. They're going out of their way to keep me quiet.*

ANNA: At the federal level it ceased operating properly. It went into this corporate miasma and started operating, not only ON the jurisdiction of the Sea, but IN the jurisdiction of the Sea. Our land based Constitution was set aside.

Now, it wasn't in any way, harmed — it did not loose its validity — in fact it had to be in place in order for them to succeed to the service part of the contract. OK? That original Constitution was called — *and let's go over his very slowly* — The Constitution for the united States of America.

And it was a capital "T" on the article "The" and it was a small "f" on the "for" and a small "u" on the "united". And if you look at that carefully, you will see that "The" used in this way means that there is only one, and you also see that "united" was used as an adjective to describe the states of America. The actual parties to the Constitution are the unincorporated states of America; "united" was just an adjective describing their joint mutual action in support of the Constitution.

Now, the word "constitution" has no particular magic to it. The legal meaning of "constitution" is that it is a debt agreement, and in this case it was the debt that the states of America, individually and together, assumed when they ordered these 19 enumerated services from the newly created federal government.

OK. So that's all the Constitution really means is that there is an agreement here, and these are the duties, and the people responsible for paying for the services, and for the performance of those duties. All Right?

So, you can have any number of constitutions, and indeed we do. In 1848 the corporation operating as the United States of America, Inc., published its Constitution called the Constitution of the United States of America. OK? So, that is not the same as the origianal Constituton which is a tri-lateral international treaty. What was published in 1868 — a look alike, sound alike document — called the Constitution of the United States of America — is a corporate Charter.

Its articles are corporate articles. Its *mandments* are corporate by-laws. It looks the same and sounds the same, to an extent, but it's a different document, and a different kind of document, than the actual Constituton which underlies the whole thing.

HOSTESS: *And the one they take an Oath to today. Right?*

ANNA: No. They've gone a step beyond that even. Because the United States of America, Inc. was bankrupted in 1912. The Federal Reserve Banks came in as creditors and took it over, and they sponsored the United States of America, Inc. with a small "the" and began operating again in that business name. That doing-as-business name. Until 1933 when they bankrupted it. And that brought us to the IMF. The International Monetary Fund booted up the United

States, Inc. and operated that as the services corporation providing essential governmental services, until just recently, they went into final receivership in March, last year. [2015]

But anyway. These different services corporations have — one after another — come in as successors to contract.

Tying in our initial discussion, each one of these came back in and began providing essential governmental services, and the American people slept on. And so you started out with The United States of America, Inc. with a capital "The" that was organized by the Roman Catholic church — the Holy See — as a non-profit governmental services organization, back in 1868. It was bankrupted in 1912 and turned over to the International Banks operating the Federal Reserve System, or rather — the Federal Reserve, I should say — and then they ran up the . . .

They basically grabbed hold of our identity and abused our credit, and created the bankruptcy that led to the Great Depresssion and all of that. On purpose, because from the banker's standpoint the Great Depression was a wonderful thing. They got to put their competitors out of buniness. They got to buy labor for pennies on the dollar. They got to snap up land resourses and other businesses.

These guys were in fact, sitting over the Depression. And they did it just for their own profit. They're criminals! They're all criminals!!!

So, anyway. These people went out there, they did all this stuff, they did it all under these different "doing-business-as" names — as The United States with a capital "The", the united States of America with a small "t" on "the".

And they've even incorporated foreign countries. I mean, when you start looking into this stuff and you find out that they've been just playing this game of using and abusing our resources, and   pretending to be what they're not, and operating this game fast and loose, they have come in here and . . .

Well let me just give you an example. The Federal Reserve sponsored the United States of America, Inc. with a small "the", and they bankrupted it in 1933 and 1934, and part of that, as you'll see in the Emergency Bankruptcy Act of 1934 and in HJR 192 and elsewhere, they set up a fixed exchange rate for their private currency script known as Federal Reserve Notes.

Now what's a note? Well, it's a "promissory note", it's an I.O.U.. So they printed these things, these Federal Reserve Notes, which are the private "promissory notes" of a banking cartel. All Right?

And they charged us for the privilege of our "use" of these private script notes, which are just I.O.U.s, and then they set up this exchange rate that was fixed. It was a dollar for dollar exchange rate. It was their script, their intrinsically useless paper promises, against our United States dollars which were defined as an ounce of fine silver.

So they were able to trade their "paper promises to pay" for our actual gold and silver, and in this way they emptied Fort Knox and by 1971 they had stolen all our silver reserves, too.

And then they declared bankruptcy when it came time for them to pay back for all these promissory notes. Right? They declared bankruptcy and they named our Estates as their sureties.

So they not only stole us blind and then used bankruptcy protection, they also named us as the ones responsible for their debts. That is what has gone on in the country. That was the 1933 Bankruptcy, and now we're in the midst of dealing with the IMF's United States, Incorporated, trying to do the same thing.

HOSTESS: *Well they do this you know. We're talking about all those programs they're implementing with FRNs when all of a sudden they offer these grants, they offer these huge grants for public health people and for sheriff's departments, and for all of these institutions to do these horrible things to the public.*

So where is this grant money coming from?

ANNA: It's coming from racketeering and theft. OK?

You have to understsand that what they setup was a fiat money system. It's a debt-credit money system. Everytime you pay some-body, you give them your debt. So every time a debt is created, an equal credit is created — it's unavoidable. So when they talk about the National Debt; what happened to the National Credit?

OK. It's their National Debt to us. It's our National Credit against them. We are their priority creditors. All right? So they owe us all this money that they can never hope to repay. They owe us all this work that they siphoned off. They owe us all the materials that they siphoned off. $18 Trillion dollars worth! OK?

So that's the actual fact.

But all of this was done in our names, with them, the very perpetrators of this whole scheme, claiming to be our representatives, and we were the victims of the scheme.

And it was all accomplished by fraud.

Well in fraud, there is no statute of limitations. It doesn't matter if you discovered that the fraud was 150 years ago, as we have, you can still come back and claim against any fraud, and you can still sue for the probate of any estate.

Fraud, and the statute of limitation and probate, never closes. An Heir to an estate can come back 150-250 years later, and if they have a valid claim, they can lay claim to an estate.

So, these are the things that operate in our favor, and before I overwhelm everybody with depression and fear, and desperation and panic here, because, you know, yes, this has happend three times before, and they're trying to pull it again. The appropriate objections have been raised, and they have been raised in the right places.

So that's number One. They tried to do an end run around the Constitution and just open up our borders, and basically tried to kick us. They basically tried to destroy America. And the way they did it, is that they let the United States, Inc. — the IMF let the United States, Inc. go into receivership without naming a secondary — without naming anyone or anything to act as successor to contract. That left the federal side of the Constitution contract flapping in the wind. Vacated, like everything else.

So, we came in and formed a partnership, an agreement, with the American Indian Nations, which are federal entities. And that sealed up the Constitution again, until such time as everybody gets back in the saddle and reforms the land government that we're owed, and can begin dealing with these large problems and this huge amount of criminality that we have suffered. We have in that capacity made several moves and one of them is to repudiate the "odeous debt" that has been accumulated by both the Federal Reserve and the IMF against the American people and against our assets.

An "odeous debt", as explained in our "Affidavit of Probable Cause", which is published as a book called, "You Know Something Is Wrong When...: An American Affidavit of Probable Cause" which is available on AMAZON.com.

An "odious debt" is a debt which is created by fraud from which the victims do not benefit. And the American people have been victims. We have been enslaved. We have been "press-ganged". We've been suffered "inland piracy". We have suffered "unlawful "conversion". We have suffered Sedition against our lawful government. We have suffered Treason. And there is no doubt about it. But we are not guilty, and we are not ignorant. We were deliberately kept in the dark so as to facilitate the criminal tresspass against us and against our government.

So all the while that we have been blissfully unaware of all these changes and machinations behind our back, we cannot be held accountable for any of that. And now that we know the truth, we are responsible for owning up and governing ourselves and being self-governed.

Well we have to do the job. We have to get our own government on the land back up and in order and operating as expeditiously as possible. And we can be helped in that by the efforts of a group of people in Michigan who, back at the time when the bankruptcy of the United States of America, Inc. was settled in 1999, realized that they had to make claim on the land and its assets. They had to reinstitute their land based government or loose it.

So these people in Michigan formed the "Michigan General Jural Society", and they organized their counties on the land, and they elected the people to fill the vacant public offices, and they placed their claim with the World Court at the Hague.

So, they placed their claim in the proper places, and they also gave notice in the Wall Street Journal and other publications around the world. And because the State of Michigan got its act together, they put their foot in the door, and preserved the claim for all the other states under the equal footing doctrine: *"What's good for one, is good for all."*

And we're all in that contract. So Michigan saved our bacon. And at the same time, they also began the effort to try to get other states and other counties to organize, and the end result is that they have bequeathed to us the precious opportunity, and a grounding to continue our claim to be the United States of America, and to retain our jurisdiction on the land.

HOSTESS: *What happened in Michigan, and the equal-footing doctrine. All that is good news, Anna.*

ANNA: I'd heard about it at the time that it happened. I just read the "big five release" and because of them I realized that that needed to happen. And it did happen, and thank God, because it kept our claim alive, and it's keeping our claim alive and giving us the basis to come back and deal with the current situation; even though so many of our counties are still not organized and our states, generally speaking, are either just hobbling along on a skeleton crew, or not organized at all.

So Job One is to fill the vacant public offices. And we all know, basically, how to hold elections. So it's not really such a hard job. You have to be able to explain what has happened to people, so they're aware, and they know why they have to go through this process. And why they have to serve as volunteers, for now, and why they have to be willing and able to assert their correct political status. But it's really not that difficult.

You basically know that you need these county officers. You need assemblymen and assemblywomen to conduct the business of the county. You need judges to run the county courts and justices of the peace to run the county courts. You need a bailiff, a land recorder, a clerk of the county, a clerk of the court, a bailiff, a coroner. These are all basic county offices, and it's going to seem kind of odd because of course, for the time being, to have these people running another county under the same or very similar name, and it will appear that they're doing the same job, but they're not, as I explained to the sheriff.

The sheriff on the land is the peace-keeping officer, with the actual public office and the actual authority of the public office, whereas their sheriffs on the sea are operating the corporate office as just a private corporate officer with a governmental services contract owed to the corporation as a franchise, which is just to enforce the codes and statutes and regulations of the corporation.

HOSTESS: *You can go into their meetings, you know, Anna, and I've done it, and you quickly understand that you are a guest at their business meeting. And they treat you that way. They allow you to speak for 3 minutes, they don't comment on anything you say, and then they move on as if you've said nothing. And this is going on across the country. If the people* *doubt this, just attend the County Commissioner's meetings, or our School Board meetings, and you can watch. That's what's happening.*

ANNA: Well, and now you know what's happening, and how it got started. And who we are dealing with, and who is in back of all of this. You've got, the Federal Reserve Banks have reconstituted themselves under the auspices of the United Nations City State, and they are operating the FEDERAL RESERVE under that municiple law, and they have made a bond to become the successors to contract, which we've rebutted and rebuffed.

HOSTESS: *You explained a lot of this in the article you wrote "The End of 400 years of Meddling and Predation in America" and it's on anticorruptionsociaty.com. I posted it as "America Free At Last".*

ANNA: Well basically, we've discovered the process of what it takes to reclaim you're true political status, and to reconvey your estate and your home back off from the jurisdiction of the Sea, and back onto the land, and to place it in your control so that they cannot mess with you. Which is a wonderful thing. And this has just happened very recently and we are very quickly moving to get the process perfected, and to get the news out to people so that millions of Americans can "come home".

The other thing that has happened just in the last couple of weeks is that we have finally figured out how to invoke the "bounty-hunter clause" of the 14th Amendment — of *their* 14th Amendment I should say — the *corporation's* 14th Amendment.

Now, remember that I told you that the IMF doing business as the United States, Inc. went basically completely insolvent in March of 2015. OK? So they are in receivership and are being liquidated by Swiss Banks. So in the meantime, the Federal Reserve — newly constituted as I said before break — has come forward doing business as THE UNITED STATES OF AMERICA and they're making a bid to operate as successor to contract even though we have formally rebuffed them and refused their service except as a voluntary act on their part. So now we've got the United States of America back in here, and we've got the Federal Reserve back in here acting as the actual service provider of government services. All Right?

Well, their corporate Constitution is the one that they published in 1868. And there is no other. So they're still obligated — if they're going to operate in the public, they're still obligated to operating under the old federal code, and they're still operating under that Constitution, the Constitution of the United States of America that was published in 1868.

Now, if you look at that very closely, you're going to see some very weird things. You're going to see the 13th Amendment, which proclaimed the Abolition of Slavery, doesn't actually abolish slavery. It actually enshrines slavery and makes it a part of their government, forever. The 13th Amendment actually says it abolishes slavery except that criminals can be enslaved. And then it leaves it up to the Congress to detemine who a criminal is, or what criminality is.

The Congress could make a law that says that "breathing" was criminal and use that as a means to enslave everyone. They actually used that as a means to make a claim for their corporation and for themselves, absolute despotism. All right? So that's the first thing that you will notice.

The second thing that you will notice as you go down the page, is the 14th Amendment in which they gratuitously confer the status of "United States Citizen" on everyone. Now this is the basis of their presumption against you and your estate, and your name. They just arbitrarily said, "Oh! You're all part of our Casino. You're all Employees. You are all obliged and obligated to us." And this new "Person" that we're creating, this "Thing" that has been named after you at the federal level, is "guilty" by definition, and it is a "slave" by definition, and it cannot even question the public debt. Now this is the all-capital-letters name. This is the federal level Trust that they created in the 14th Amendment.

So, when a court brings a charge against the all-capital-letters name, that public trust is being created without your knowledge and consent, without your parents knowledge and consent, without your grandparents knowledge and consent. That entity is already guilty. It's already a debtor. All that's left to talk about is how much it's going to pay. And that's what you see in their courtrooms today.

Now, the other interesting thing is when they pull this kind of crap on people in commercial venues, they have to give remedy at the same time. So your remedy is also in the 14th Amendment, and that is the Bounty-hunter Clause. And that is also right there in front of you. The Bounty-hunter Clause has been a course of debate and concern and people have scratched their heads for generations as to what all that was really about, and how it could be accessed as a remedy for 14th Amendment citizens.

We finally cracked it. We finally know the process by which people can invoke the Bounty-hunter Clause so that their own court of record can go in there and get remedy. The very first case resulted in a $68 Million dollar judgement in favor of the man who did his, and four [4] big law firms were put out of business. Approximately sixty [60] lawyers lost their BAR cards.

Yes. And they are now all facing federal criminal charges. But there is a gag order on this because the guy who did it doesn't want the notariety. He has a family to protect. But the information — the process — is being fully detailed and it's going to be employed all across this country. The details of it — the process — will be made public. It will be made available to anyone, and every one who has suffered at the hands of these monsters.

The BAR Associations are about to get their own "come-up-ance" according to their own rules. And not just with coming liens, but with actual criminal charges against people — against BAR members who do this kind of stuff to people. Who have acted as Predators and as Pirates on our shores. This is very serious and it is a remedy.

This is great news for us, but not so great news for them.

The presumption is that they're all acting as 14th Amendment Citizens — "PERSONS". As persons they are "Subjects", they're not sovereign, they are subject to the whims of the corporation. So when the corporate legislature lays down its almighty hand, then you have to jump if you're a member of that corporation, and if you're enfranchised as a voter, and all this "offer me" happy horse hockey (you know what) and what they're saying is absolutely true. If you bought into this, and this is what you agreed to, and you're a good corporate tool, well then, you have to do everything they tell you to do. Because that's what you agreed to by contract.

However, if you're not — if you're one of the free and sovereign independent people of the United States, and you're not an inhabitant, or British Subject, or subject of the Municipality of the District of Columbia, or a "PERSON", which means a corporation in Federal-ese, then you are outside of all that, you are exempt. Your are literally exempt from all such requirements. And that's the truth they're not telling you.

They're talking exclusively to Persons. To those who have accepted their fate as corporate entities, these franchises of these corporations. And if you agree and consent to be a Person, those are your rules. If you don't, then they're not your rules. These rules are for legal fiction Persons. Sixty [60] of them were put out of business in just one action. And there are people working on the big picture.

The land jurisdiction is coming back.

And the land jurisdiction has its authority formally vested in the international law of the sea, as well as on the land. We're coming back after those rats, those criminals.

In the international jurisdiction of the sea we're going to bring them to trial as war criminals and see absolute relief and restitution that the victims of this are owed. So the answer to the whole thing is coming.

Ordinary people acting in the public interest can destroy these corporations. They're just corporations. They're subject to dissolution and liquidation.

If they act outside their charters, they act in a criminal manner. They can be liquidated right down to their eye-teeth. And every corporate officer has no public office; they have no immunity.

They chose the Nuremberg Defense: "Oh! I was just following orders."

"As It Is The Truth!"

4
Where the Bear Went, and Where We Are

On Jul 18, 2014 The Archbishop of Chicago, Cardinal Francis Eugene George, wrote to Anna von Reitz:

> I stand with the universal Catholic Church founded by Christ. All the people whom you accuse of defrauding American citizens were elected by American citizens. That doesn't mean that what they do is morally right, but the responsibility, finally rests with the Electorate.
>
> God bless you.
> Francis Cardinal George, O.M.I.
> Archbishop of Chicago"

THE FOLLOWING RESPONSE was sent by Anna Maria Wilhelmina Hanna Sophia: Riezinger-von Reitzenstein von Lettow a.k.a. Ann von Reitz of Big Lake Alaska:

My Dear Archbishop George,

I, too, stand with the universal Catholic Church, founded by Christ. My blood seal stands upon the record of the Vatican Chancery Court in Witness of what I am going to show you tonight. I am from a family that has served the Catholic Church since the First Holy Roman Empire, Hereditary Grand Marshals of the Holy Roman Empire, Knights of the Holy Sepulcher. I have myself served as an International Services Agent and as a private attorney in service to his Holiness Pope Benedict XVI and now, Pope Francis.

You must believe that I am in deadly earnest both about the seriousness of the criminality engulfing America and the danger this poses to the Church and to the Rule of Law.

The Canon Law of the Church stands above every other form of law, and the Roman Curia above all other courts.

Even the Uniform Commercial Code which was developed by the Curia as a just means to resolve the many international disputes and claims arising from the 1930 bankruptcies of the G-5 nations is copyrighted by Unidroit, a subsidiary of the Vatican.

The organization which failed and which plunged America into this desperate criminality was originally chartered by the Church as a religious non-profit corporation.

We, Sir, are up to our ears in culpability for the circumstance herein discussed, and both the Pope Emeritus and Pope Francis have duly considered all the issues, and acting in their temporal capacities have rendered judgment as international Trustees of The United States Trust (1789) recognizing the Breach of Trust and the criminality which has been practiced against the American States and the American State Citizens.

They have both taken strong action to begin addressing the circumstance.

Pope Benedict XVI acted to create a new office in the Postal Service, establishing a regional Postmaster for North America.

Pope Francis has issued his First Apostolic Letter, the Motu Proprio of July 11, 2013, rewriting the international criminal code as part of his continuing effort to address this situation, and has more recently addressed the United Nations and collapsed the worldwide derivatives market.

This is not about any "responsibility" of the electorate. It is about the Church's responsibility to support the Pope in his role as the Ultimate Trustee of the Global Estate, to uphold the Rule of Law, and to make correction for a grave Breach of Trust that continued for 165 years and which has cost millions of innocent lives.

We can only confess our sins, dear Cardinal, admitting as mere mortals our desperate need for grace and rising up each day to do what we can and must.

I direct your attention to the Treaty of Paris which ended the American Revolution and the corollary Treaty of Versailles.

There are three international Trustees named as Caretakers of The United States Trust (1789). They are the Pope in His Temporal Office, the British Monarch, and The United States Postmaster (Civil).

Now I direct your attention to the Treaty of Westminster (1794) in which the City State of Westminster and the Crown Temple pledged "amity" in "perpetuity" with the newly formed United States.

Next, I direct your attention to the Treaty of Verona (1845) in which the then-Pope and the British Monarch, both Trustees of the American national trust, agreed that the representative form of government was incompatible with Divine Right of Kings and with Papal Supremacy, and so both acted in secretive Breach of Trust.

The British Monarch issued Letters of Marque and Reprisal to the members of the Bar Association (British Crown Commercial Company) which issued licenses to privateers to attack American "vessels" in international jurisdictions of the law. That, Sir, is the genesis of Bar Association Licenses.

A "license" as you must know, is permission to engage in an act which would otherwise be illegal.

The Americans responded by quickly passing an Amendment to their Constitution effectively barring attorneys from holding public office.

In 1860, Abraham Lincoln, a Bar attorney, was elected President of the United States (Commercial Company) but could not lawfully act as the President of The United States of America (Major).

This is why representatives of eleven Southern States refused to be seated and left the Congress adjourned sine die.

In 1863, Lincoln was forced to bankrupt the original Trust Management Company doing business as The United States.

After years of bankruptcy reorganization known euphemistically as "reconstruction" a new Trust Management Organization was incorporated by the Church, doing business as the United States of America, Inc. This entity operated under Church auspices from the end of the Reconstruction to 1912, when the Trust Management Organization was purchased by a consortium of banks doing business as the Federal Reserve.

By 1913 they had pushed through the "Federal Reserve Act" and via legal tender laws began a purposeful agenda to devalue the American Dollar and bankrupt the original corporation doing business as the United States of America, Inc.

In May of 1930, the G-5 nations declared international bankruptcy via joint treaty entered into at the Geneva Conventions. Franklin Delano Roosevelt was the representative of the Federal Reserve dba United States of America, Inc.

Three years later, having been elected President, he declared domestic bankruptcy as well.

One of his first acts was to illegally confiscate privately held American gold, which was never repaid.

As the United States of America, Inc. was being prepared for bankruptcy, agents throughout the Congress and the individual states of the Union rushed through a process of "registering franchises".

They created "states of states" merely named after the actual geographically defined American states. They also created foreign situs trusts named after each and every living American.

At the March 6, 1933, Conference of Governors meeting, the Governors — merely corporate officers of franchises of the bankrupt United States of America, Inc. — pledged the *"good faith and credit"* of *"their States and the citizenry thereof"* to stand as sureties for the debts of the United States of America, Inc., during its bankruptcy reorganization.

Imagine that Burger King International went bankrupt in the UK, and it called all the local franchise owners together and they all agreed to name their customers as sureties for their corporate debts.

This is what happened in America in 1933. And the victims were not told a word about this.

The perpetrators were rewarded by the bankers with access to virtually unlimited credit "hypothecated" against the assets of the American States and the private property of the American State Citizens.

All this credit cost the bankers nothing material, as they had inculcated a fiat money system. Issuing credit — "money of account" — cost them nothing but the time involved to enter digits in an account ledger.

In exchange for this favor to the politicians, the bankers were rewarded with legal tender laws allowing this clever "system" to exist in America, and were given surreptitious title to all real property assets in America, and provided with protection for their activities by the members of the Bar Associations.

In 1944, FDR quit claimed all the juicy service contracts and the assets used to service these governmental service contracts to the IMF.

The IMF took over from the Federal Reserve, gaining control of every logo, name, title, department, and agency of the "United States of America, Inc."— what Americans believe to be their government — right down to the American flag.

They charted a new Trust Management Organization in France doing business as the UNITED STATES, Inc., and moved in.

They also took over the "State" franchises and opened their own "STATE OF_____" franchises.

For the past 70 years they have enslaved the people of America and plundered the assets of The United States Trust (1789).

The creditors who forced the bankruptcy of the United States of America, Inc., included the World Bank, the International Bank of Development and Reconstruction, and the Federal Reserve — but the priority creditors named in the 1934 Bankruptcy Act were the American States and the American State Citizens.

The banks, being aware of their own schemes, named the Secretary of the Treasury of Puerto Rico to act as their chosen Bankruptcy Trustee. (See Federal Title 5 for details.)

The Secretary of the Treasury of Puerto Rico seized all the bogus "States on Paper" and "Americans on Paper" created by the Roosevelt Administration and rolled all the assets presumed to be part of these trusts into Roman Inferior Trusts (Cestui Que Vie Trusts) operated "in the NAME of" the foreign situs trusts Roosevelt created.

Thus, a living man denoted properly as "john quincy adams" was misrepresented as a foreign situs trust doing business as "John Quincy Adams" and then this entity was declared "dead, presumed missing at sea" by the perpetrators of this massive identity theft scheme, and all the assets of "John Quincy Adams" were rolled over into a Roman Inferior Trust doing business as "JOHN QUINCY ADAMS".

The Secretary of the Treasury of Puerto Rico also "removed" all these Roman Inferior Trusts to Puerto Rico for "safe keeping" where they came under the foreign jurisdiction of the Puerto Rican

Commonwealth and the UK. There they were enslaved and taxed for the privilege of **importing revenue** to Puerto Rico — otherwise known as the "**in**come tax".

All this was done in the name of winning World War II.

The claims against the American assets supplied the credit to boot up the war industry effort, and seizing the ESTATES of the Americans and "redefining" individual Americans as chattel belonging to their own ESTATES allowed a means of conscripting millions of men into the Armed Services.

After the War, nothing changed. The perpetrators never retooled American industry for peace.

They just went on pumping out armaments and selling arms and borrowing money against assets they never owned, and enslaving the American people to the tune of Yankee Doodle Dandy.

Over the years the criminality of the arms dealers has become a terrible worldwide problem.

They branched out from simply selling weapons and promoting war, to selling drugs and running gambling and prostitution rings, booze and cigarettes, and every form of vice, violence, and viciousness.

They also used their position of trust as "the government" to manipulate commodity and stock markets, and control natural resources belonging to the American people for private gain.

And the Church is culpable, because at the broader base, the Church knew about it and did nothing. It continued to mindlessly operate on the directives established by the Treaty of Verona and never re-examined the disastrous consequences of all this for humanity, much less the hideous theft and abuse practiced upon the Americans — incalculable amounts of labor siphoned off, incalculable material losses, and millions of lives lost or maimed in wars for profit.

By Judge Anna von Reitz   107

To that, you and your peers have turned a blind eye and shrugged, and said, it's the responsibility of the voters.

The same voters who have been purposefully misled and self-interestedly abused, kept in the dark, manipulated, defrauded, and robbed. By their EMPLOYEES, and those they trusted to act in their behalf. By the Supreme Pontiff, who was obligated by solemn treaty to act as their Trustee.

It's with good reason that the higher administrators of the Church have been reluctant to expose the criminality or deal with it, for fear that the Church would be blamed.

However, by 2009, the Church was being blamed, effectively and determinedly, until it was all finally brought before Pope Benedict XVI, who accepted responsibility, who exercised his temporal powers, and began dealing with the corruption.

Pope Francis has brought the vitality and vigor and insight needed to the Office and is continuing to bring remedy.

Meanwhile the bankruptcy of the United States of America, Inc., has finally been ended.

The old "Federal Reserve System" is no more, but a new version of "FEDERAL RESERVE" has been organized under UNITED NATIONS auspices and has tried to mount a new round of the same old game in collusion with the IMF.

It's a funny thing about a "debt-credit" monetary system. When you create a *debt,* for one party, you unavoidably create a *credit,* for another.

So when people talk about the "National Debt" being "$13 or $21 or however many trillion "dollars", that means that somewhere, someone or something, is being CREDITED with that amount of money.

Exactly who and what came to the surface in July of 2011.

"As It Is The Truth!"

We have the UCC Filings on file.

The perpetrators rolled the credit side of the "National Debt" over into the "United States Department of the Treasury" and used it to back a new specie of fiat debt note called "US TREASURY NOTES". They have attempted, in other words, to initiate another round of the same old scam.

There is little doubt that it was the intention of the two colluding banking cartels — the FEDERAL RESERVE and the IMF — to simply reverse positions: bankrupt the UNITED STATES, INC., leaving the Roman Inferior Trusts named after the Americans to stand as sureties for the debts of the insolvent UNITED STATES, INC. during another nice, long bankruptcy reorganization.

Intervention by Pope Benedict XVI and Pope Francis both, together with ever-increasing public awareness of the situation and the fraud, has served to make what is euphemistically called "**re**-venue" impossible.

In addition to the American State Citizens waking up, the Russians and Chinese and other nations of the BRICS Alliance woke up.

As part of the fraud practiced against the Americans, Canadians, Australians, Japanese, and the populations of most of the countries of Western Europe, all bank accounts were converted over to the ownership of the banks.

As you now know, if you didn't before, all bank accounts belonging to "JOHN QUINCY PUBLIC" are in fact accounts belonging to a Puerto Rican ESTATE Trust owned and operated by agencies of the IMF.

This is how Christine LaGarde can speak so nonchalantly about seizing American 401k's and savings and other retirement accounts: the IMF surreptitiously owns those accounts.

The living Americans who innocently deposited their life savings into those accounts thinking that they were their own private personal bank accounts have been deceived and defrauded and "presumed" by the perpetrators to "donate" everything in those accounts to "public trusts" operated in their NAMES.

Remember — I am an officer of the Church, too.

I have taken the vow and placed the blood seal on the altar.

This is not a joke.

This is not a rehearsal.

Take what you believe to be "your" check book out of your pocket and a strong magnifying glass and look at what appears to be the signature line — what do you see?

It's not really a line.

It's a row of microprint endlessly repeating "authorizing signature, authorizing signature".

Why would that verbiage have to be there, and why would it have to be obscured? To keep the victims from knowing the truth — that all their assets in banks have been unlawfully converted over to the ownership of the banks.

You've already been told about the Puerto Rican ESTATE Trusts. Now witness the IRS scam.

The living man, "john quincy adams", is exempt by law from ever having to pay taxes, and by definition, "income" is profit accrued by corporations.

Therefore, it is literally impossible for any living American to owe an income tax, yet millions upon millions of Americans are robbed, defrauded, harassed, and even imprisoned over "income" taxes every year.

How is this possible?

The JOHN QUINCY ADAMS ESTATE is a trust, a legal fiction entity, a corporation.

Every **dime** that the living man known as "john quincy adams" unknowingly "donates" to the bank account belonging to the JOHN QUINCY ADAMS ESTATE is 100% profit for a Puerto Rican trust, and it just so happens that there is an **excise tax** for the privilege of **importing revenue** to Puerto Rico. The monster taxes the poor devils for the privilege of **giving them** their money, and then people like Christine LaGarde sit around drinking champagne callously discussing exactly how to finesse the seizure of the retirement accounts of millions of innocent American Senior Citizens.

But there are worse things.

Other elements, among the criminals, have taken out million dollar life insurance policies on every American man, woman and child.

They think they will simply murder a few hundred million of their creditors and collect on the life insurance policies.

Have you not heard of the **"All Seeing"**? Cardinal George?

I am the left hand of **"anu:hotep"** and I will be obeyed in this matter, as will Pope Francis.

There will be no seizure of the American retirement accounts, no false flags, no murder, no mayhem, no scalar weapons deployed.

There will be no deceptive "offers" in commerce seeking to exchange gold for land or human capital under conditions of nondisclosure and deceit.

There will be an end to this criminality and to the complacency of the Church and of the American Cardinals and Archbishops responsible for the mis-administration of the courts.

Or there will be Hell on earth, Cardinal George — literally, and it will not come against the innocent Americans. The Left Hand of God will come for those who are responsible and unrepentant.

The Treaty of Verona is extinguished.

All Bar Association licenses are extinguished.

By order of Pope Francis, all attorneys, all clerks, every member of the judicial system operating these frauds and oppressions became 100% individually and commercially liable as of September 1, 2013, past.

The banking cartels and governmental services corporations have been given three years [September 2016] to clean up their acts from top to bottom, to come into compliance with the Original Equity contract owed to the Americans, and to stop operating in criminal default.

I suggest that you get over your idea that it is the voter's responsibility.

May God bless you to the same extent that you bless others.

Anna Maria Wilhelmina Hanna Sophia: Riezinger-von Reitzenstein von Lettow

5
Please Pray For Mainstreet

I have spent the day pouring through piles of correspondence—answered what I could, and despaired of the rest. My helpers have done their best to sort mail into piles and with any luck donations for the Living Law Firm and the 50 States Claim have been gleaned out and distributed to the many who need support to continue their work.

As always I am overwhelmed with the misery and the vast numbers of innocent Americans who have been silently, day after day, preyed upon—- property stolen, lives ruined, years spent in prison, all under the guise of law and order and the American Way.

Read Psalm 119: 105-178, if you would commune with me tonight. This is my outcry tonight and the outcry of all those who have not forgotten His Ways and His Commands, who remember what the Law really is and is supposed to be, as opposed to this horrible corporate sham.

I am here to tell you that the United States— our "neighbor" headquartered in the District of Columbia — has been the author of this misery and the cause and the reason from Day One. While pretending to work with us and for us, it has done anything and everything to undermine, steal from, and ruin America. Both the British and the French Governments and those backing their Central Banks are responsible, as are the Vatican agents who have stood mum and profited and looked the other way.

Let the Truth and the Fruits guide your way. If any man, cause, or religion would have your allegiance, let them prove worthy with thought, word, and deed.

We all bear a part of the responsibility and own a share of the fact that things have come to this, a time when we have had the rankest kinds of criminals running our government and presiding over our courts. We have not done our part. We have been asleep at the wheel. We've been here and yet not present, lulled into a dull and deadly complacency, fooled by political parties and sideshows, brand names and semantic deceits, thinking that someone named "George" could do it all for us, though he has been dead for over 200 years. I still run into that every day— someone wanting to rant at me under the assumption that it is my job— and not theirs— to run the actual American government.

To the extent that our government exists or has ever existed, it is an inner government that begins with ourselves; it exists in our determination to govern ourselves and to do so according to high principles, to choose those principles with discernment and to join with others in pursuit of their manifestation on Earth: we hold these Truths to be self-evident….that all men are created equal.

Today, it has been announced that massive bounties payable in gold are being offered for the arrest of former leaders of this country. There can be no doubt that mercenaries from around the world will flock like crows, eager to waylay such familiar figures as the Bush Family and President Obama. That these false leaders are guilty of many sins and omissions cannot be disputed, yet in my opinion, the true problem goes much deeper and lies in fact not with these kings, but with the king-makers, who are now offering these people up as sacrifices for their own sins.

Ask yourselves— who has a ton of gold to offer as such a reward, and who would answer the call to claim such a reward? Only members of the Illuminati, the Pope, the Queen, a few foreign governments have tons of gold to give away. Only bounty hunters will answer, violent commercial mercenaries motivated by such things as gold and now they will be "in action" on our shores, prowling around in quiet hamlets like Crawford, Texas. And the local police will have to do battle with them.

All those who are celebrating this action by the "White Dragon Society" think again. A form of gangland style war has begun on our shores, without any big news announcement, without any vote from Congress. And we must ask ourselves——why?

Our failure to arrest these people and hold them accountable ourselves is the root of all of this. It should have happened years and years ago. We should have arrested the entire remaining Congress after the Civil War and charged them with treason. The Army dawdled, concerned about their pay— then as now—and we slept on.

We should have arrested those who passed the Federal Reserve Act and executed them for treason.

We should have arrested FDR instead of electing him for four terms.

We should have and we would have, if we had known, but we mistook the "United States" as part of ourselves and so it has continued on its destructive, venal course, and we reap the inevitable truth that when you fail to govern yourself, somone else is eventually forced to do it for you.

I don't doubt that Comey's failure to indict Hillary Clinton and Jacob Rothschild's attempts to play still more games in France have been the final straws mandating all of this. Perhaps, too, our recent Estate Claim Letter laying bare the history of the Holy See's former involvement and present responsibility with respect to the ongoing criminality of our court system and banking system has proded certain parties into action.

So now we have foreign mercenaries of every kind and stripe coming to Mainstreet, America.

The very best thing that could happen would be for those named to voluntarily enter into protective custody and to remain in protective custody pending trial. In this way, the whole situation could be diffused and lives could be saved. The second option, which would also be acceptable, would be for our own police and military to arrest the miscreants pending trial. It might be too little and too late, but at least we would be taking responsibility and enforcing order on what will happen anyway.

Tonight, please accept my special thanks to all those men who stepped forward in support of our 50 States Claim and all those who have sent donations to me, purchased our book, and supported the Living Law Firm. We can't possibly respond to the sheer volume of correspondence, but you can be sure that we hear and we care and we are doing everything we can to restore honesty in banking and government and justice to the courts.

This is a battle no less than any other battle and we are against vast and evil forces. Our poor country is still struggling with issues left over from the Civil War, but we must all place our lamps on a lamp stand and let them be burning brightly even so—and each of us, according to our own insights and talents must take up our part.

"As It Is The Truth!"

6

They Stole Our Names.... And Now They've Lost Them

What I am going to tell you all today is going to blow your minds— if they aren't staggered already.

First, the rats under FDR pretended that our Trade Names, the Upper and Lower Case names we were taught to use in grade school styled like this: Felix Morton Morganthau —- were actually Foreign Situs Trusts belonging to the "Federal Government" doing business as the United States of America (Inc.) and represented franchises of that bankrupt private, mostly foreign owned governmental services corporation.

So, those entrusted to act as public servants instead acted as public hogs and placed false claims against the American nation-states and the American People. And our parents and grandparents were so trusting they didn't catch on.

Year after year, they toiled away, paying debts for crooks—debts they never owed. They didn't even get a thank you for it. The perpetrators snuck off with their buddies in the Beltway and snickered to themselves and patted themselves on the back and sucked up and siphoned off the wealth of America while sending our young men and women off to war for profits—and not even profits for themselves, but profits for the perpetrators of these abuses.

So they stole our names and bankrupted them and now, they've lost all record of them.

You have to go back to court and do an adult name change from FELIX MORTON MORGANTHAU back to Felix Morton Morganthau.

Even worse, they've done the same thing with the States.

Where does this bunko stop? Where in the name of Jesus does it end?

You have to adopt your own given Name and then you have to seize upon and reconvey the bogus franchise trust NAMES, too. And Expatriate them. And bring suit against the rats in the proper venue.

And you have to do this to save yourselves and your country.

Do you hate this situation yet? Do you feel betrayed yet?

You've been subjected to the greatest fraud and identity theft in human history and the people you have relied upon to protect you and your interests and paid well to do so—— are the ones that have done this to you and yours.

If you aren't righteously angry enough to get up off your couch and start talking and walking, too, then I don't know what I can say to you.

7

"Where Is The Mandate?"

Years ago there was a wonderful TV commercial with a feisty old woman who looked at her puny fast food sandwich, wrinkled her nose and spouted, "Where's the beef?"

Now you've got another feisty old lady saying, "Where's the mandate?"

You've all learned that the United States is not America. You've learned that, most likely, you aren't a "United States Citizen" nor a "citizen of the United States", either. You've learned that their elections aren't our elections. You've learned that they are not the actual government of this country— just a foreign jurisdictional enclave and a corporation under contract to provide us and our Several States of the Union with "essential governmental services"——Well, there is something else you have to think about now.

All your life you have heard it endlessly repeated: "Democracy, Democracy, Democracy….. as if "democracy" were some great thing and we were proud to be a "democracy"——but America was never a "democracy". The 50 nation states are all Republics, and republics are very, very different from democracies.

Republics honor and protect each one of the people. Democracies have no respect for you or your rights at all. They function by Mob Rule— whatever the majority wants, the majority gets.

So, if 51% of your neighbors want to eat you for Christmas Dinner, that's okay in a "democracy." If they want to steal your land, that's okay, too. If they want to rape your daughters or your house guests like in old Sodom and Gemorrah, well, what do you think?

Democracy — *Demon-crazy.*

Your country–meaning your state of the Union— is not a "democracy" and you certainly don't want to spread "democracy" around the world.

But there is one thing about a "democracy"—- it requires a "majority" to work, and without a majority, it doesn't have a mandate to act—-even according to its own profoundly disgusting rules.

Take that fact in— without a majority there is no mandate.

Now, let's do another little thought—

Only about half of the potential "voters" are registered to vote, and of those, only about 30% regularly show up at the polls, and that 30% is split roughly down the middle into two political parties, one of which will get the lion's share of votes so that at the end of the day, only about 15% of those "represented" actually get their own way—-and that number is FAR, FAR less than 50% of anything, much less a popular mandate from over half of the entire population.

It's a tiny percentage of people that are actually being represented by all these "frou-frou-rah" elections. There hasn't been an honest mandate in this country in my lifetime. So, by their own rules, and their own admissions, nothing these jokers have done has had a mandate.

None of it is lawful even under their own system.

The perpetrators have tried to excuse themselves by pretending that whatever "the majority of those who show up at the polls" wants is a mandate, but it's not.

The "demos" is the entire group of voters and they never get close to 50% of that group on one side of anything, much less any popular mandate from the public at large.

"As It Is The Truth!"

So not only have you been lied to and not only has a stinking immoral "democracy" been enabled to usurp the republican form of government you are heir to and owed, but they haven't even been able to operate a democracy lawfully.

They have no mandate. And in my lifetime they have never had a mandate. Ever.

Knowledge is power, and the ultimate civil power resides in every individual in America. By studying the links at **www.http://annavonreitz.com** in the order presented, you will know more about freedom and what the creator expected from us and endowed us with, Through His Divine Son, and you will know your responsibility in that regard.

Notice to Congress —
The Days of Legalizing Theft Are Over

From the writings of Judge Anna von Reitz. Big Lake Alaska September 2014

The most recent round of fraud began on March 28, 1861. That was the day the Congress of the united States of America adjourned for lack of quorum and never reconvened. Ever since, "Congress" has functioned in one of three roles—

(1) as a corporate Board of Directors for private, mostly foreign-owned and deceptively named governmental services corporations operated by banking cartels (the Federal Reserve running the "United States of America, Inc." and the IMF running the "UNITED STATES") or

(2) the government of a legislative democracy calling itself the United States of America (Minor)—American "states" more often thought of as federal territories and possessions— Guam, Puerto Rico, etc., or

(3) operating as a plenary oligarchy ruling the Washington DC Municipal Government.

All this time that you thought the members of Congress were representing you and your interests, they've been representing other interests entirely. That explains a lot, doesn't it?

On March 6, 1933 the "President" of the "United States of America, Inc.", Franklin Delano Roosevelt, attended a Conference of Governors meeting. These "Governors" were all "State" franchise managers of the United States of America, Inc., exactly like local franchise owners of Burger King or Sears. They got together and pledged the assets of their customers—their employers—the American states and people——as "sureties" for their private corporate debts. And then they bankrupted the "United States of America" and all the "State" franchises.

The "federal" States that were created by the 14th Amendment of their private for-profit corporation's look-alike, sound-alike "constitution" published as the "Constitution of the United States of America" are not the same as the actual States of the Union, nor are their "State" citizens the same as American State Citizens, nor are their "US citizens" the same as Citizens of the united States, but they pretended that they were and the banks gleefully agreed.

To secure the debt owed by the "United States of America, Inc." the banks established maritime salvage liens against every parcel of land, every business, every man, woman, and child in America, and continued to operate their doppelganger corporation under Chapter 11 Reorganization. They laid claim to your "good faith and credit" —stole your credit cards— and your identity as an American State Citizen, and they never bothered to tell you, the victim. They also had you declared legally dead and probated your estate and issued bonds based on the value of your labor and private property.

Just look at "your" Birth Certificate—signed by the County Registrar, an officer of the probate court, issued in the NAME of a "dead person"—you — numbered as a bond and issued on bond paper.

At the same time, they converted all your private bank accounts to the ownership of the ESTATE trust they created "in your name" and moved the ESTATE offshore to Puerto Rico where you and your assets supposedly came under the foreign maritime jurisdiction of the United States of America (Minor).

Look at the NAME on "your" bank account checks. Look at the

"As It Is The Truth!"

signature line under a high powered magnifier. The IMF claims that it owns all your bank accounts. It claims that your ESTATE was "abandoned", and now all the spoils belong to the bank. They are pressing "Congress" to pass "laws" to allow them to seize all American bank accounts—your savings, your retirement accounts, your checking accounts, everything.

We've seen Dodd-Frank. Now we are seeing "bail-in" proposals. The Big Banks want "Congress" to front for their greed and criminality—again. This is all fiduciary trust fraud and fiduciary trust fraud has no statute of limitations.

1862 or 1933 or 2014 — it makes no difference.

We suggest that members of Congress assume their public offices acting under full 100% individual commercial liability —or be ousted and tried as criminals. Next, we suggest that they honor their contract with America and issue debt-free public money— real American Dollars. Next, liquidate all the "too big to fail" banks, tear up the corporate charters these entities have violated, seize back our purloined assets, and shut them all down.

Meanwhile, the market for financial services will open up for banks operated under actual state charters. This thing you have thought of as your government is nothing but a multi-national conglomerate run by criminally amok. The real government of this country is vested in each of you. You all hold more civil authority on the land than the entire federal government.

Deal with the "FEDERAL RESERVE" the "IMF" and "CONGRESS" the same way you would deal with "TARGET" or "WALMART" or "ARBY'S" if they grossly endangered, cheated, enslaved, and defrauded you. Keep calm and get even. You all know what to do. You have the guaranteed Universal Right of Self-Declaration provided by United Nations Conventions, plus the protections of the Universal Declaration of Human Rights.

You have the Geneva Conventions and the Lieber Code. You have the preserved right to Common Law, guaranteed by Uniform Commercial Code 1-308 and recourse guaranteed by 1-103.6, which includes the right not to be bound by any contract that is unilateral, inequitable, involuntary, undisclosed, tainted by fraud, not in-kind, entered in your behalf by others merely claiming to represent you, or deemed to exist as the result of receiving a compelled benefit or fruit of monopoly inducement.

You have the absolute right to Expatriate from their maritime jurisdiction. Do so. When 400 million Americans stand up and clean house, the world will listen and hear the roar.

"As It Is The Truth!"

Summation

By Way of Summation to all concerned:

There are 390 million people in America and they all have problems. You are all grown ups and have to move forward together to solve the problems set before us all. We have to seek peace knowing that no peace can exist without justice.

Our diligent research of many years duration proves beyond any rational doubt that our lawful government has been usurped by "governmental services corporations" in the business of selling us -- guess what? More governmental services. In the process they have set up a web of deceits and false legal claims designed to support and expedite their racketeering and use of armed force to make us buy and pay for more and more and more "governmental services".

Obamacare is only a recent and obvious example.

The time has now come for Americans to wake up, restore their lawful government on the land, enforce the Organic and Public Law of this country and put the facts before all people, including our own.

These wrongs have been visited upon us in the international jurisdiction of the sea as a result of gross breach of trust by our international Trustee in that jurisdiction, the British Monarch, who has been in Breach of Trust with respect to the British people, the Americans, the Canadians, and the Australians for 150 years.

These are old frauds that have gone unnoticed and quietly perpetuated for generations so that they have accrued a patina of acceptability. We are told, "That's the way we do things. That's the way we've always done things." -- but according to massive amounts of public records worldwide, that simply is not true.

There are many people who have caught onto bits and pieces of this gigantic fraud and they have sounded the alarm. There are others who have misinterpreted such evidence and through ignorance have promoted their own pet theory without bothering to examine the rest of "the forest of lies" we are faced with.

My job here is to present you with the facts. Of course, I often add my own reasoning or opinion about the facts and you are welcome to disagree.

That said, I have work to do and a life to lead. I am not available to consult about individual court cases unless they present sweeping public interest issues that impact all of us.

I am also not here to argue with you about anything. If you have verifiable facts bring them forward; if not, there is no point in ranting at me as if I created this mess or am responsible for anyone else's inaction.

I am not your public servant.

I am not offering to "represent" you in any manner whatsoever apart from the fact that I am one of the "free sovereign and independent people of the United States" and whatever good I do for myself in my own behalf also accrues to all those others who are "free sovereign and independent people of the United States" by Maxim of Law and the requirements of our Organic Law which provides equal protection.

I am not a Oathkeeper nor Oath Breaker, either. I do my best to say yes or no and claim nothing more.

I am not a guru, Angel, devil, lawyer, etc., etc.,

I am a Great-grandma from Big Lake, Alaska, who can read and think like millions of other Americans and for whatever reasons -- mostly a 17 year-long battle with the IRS -- I decided to research the mess this country is in and how we got here.

The bare bones of that research and our resulting claim against the British Crown, various national governments, the American Bar Association, and at least five international banking cartels is presented in our sworn and published affidavit: *"You Know Something Is Wrong When... An American Affidavit of Probable Cause"* available on Amazon.com for around $20.

I am not involved in the marketing, printing or distribution, and receive a whopping 5% of the profit, whatever that is.

Read the affidavit and do your own due diligence to research the facts before you come to me with any assumptions.

Thank you, very much.

Judge Anna